Valentinus Basilius, Theodor Kerckring

The triumphal chariot of antimony

Valentinus Basilius, Theodor Kerckring

The triumphal chariot of antimony

ISBN/EAN: 9783337303495

Printed in Europe, USA, Canada, Australia, Japan

Cover: Foto ©Andreas Hilbeck / pixelio.de

More available books at **www.hansebooks.com**

THE

TRIUMPHAL CHARIOT
OF ANTIMONY.

BY

BASILIUS VALENTINUS.

WITH THE COMMENTARY OF

THEODORE KERCKRINGIUS,

A Doctor of Medicine.

————

BEING THE LATIN VERSION PUBLISHED AT AMSTERDAM IN THE
YEAR 1685 TRANSLATED INTO ENGLISH, WITH
A BIOGRAPHICAL PREFACE.

—— ——

London :
JAMES ELLIOTT AND CO.,
TEMPLE CHAMBERS, FALCON COURT, FLEET STREET, E.C.
—
1893.

CONTENTS.

BIOGRAPHICAL PREFACE.

SHOULD any uninstructed person who might chance upon Basil Valentine's "Triumphal Chariot of Antimony" undertake to read that work, he would probably be mystified by much of its contents, by its references to the Spagyric art, to the grand Magisterium, the true and universal Medicine, the Tinctures which transmute metals, with other unknown quantities and other deep mysteries which make part of the *Sacramentum Regis*. But if he were asked what he thought of Basil Valentine in his historical and personal character, it is unlikely that he would suppose for a moment the existence of any romantic mystery encompassing the mere life of the man. He would regard him as a pious Benedictine monk, uncommonly well versed for his period in certain departments of experimental and medical chemistry, and, perhaps, as a bizarre speculator in the cloudy borderlands of physical science ; but such biographical data as can be gathered concerning him from his writings, he would naturally accept without question, because there would be no ground for assuming any reason to doubt them. Yet even as such a person would be mistaken in his estimate of Valentine the alchemist, as distinguished from Valentine the investigator of antimonial therapeutics, so it is just possible that he would be astray in his estimate of the man, being misled by a veil of simplicity which skilfully conceals the adept under the unpretending mask of a monastic canon. "When I had emptied to the dregs the cup of human suffering, I was led to consider the wretchedness of this world," so Valentine tells us in his preface to " The Great Stone of the Sages," "and the fearful consequences of our first parents' disobedience. Then I saw that there was no hope of repentance for mankind,

that they were getting worse day by
day, and that for their impenitence God's
everlasting punishment was hanging
over them ; and I made haste to with-
draw myself from the evil world, to bid
farewell to it, and to devote myself to
the service of God." * After the manner
of his age, as he goes on to inform us, he
took refuge in a monastery, where the
time that he could spare from his de-
votions was made use of for "the study
and investigation of those natural secrets
by which God has shadowed out eternal
things." Here, in this pious retirement,
there was ultimately revealed to him
"that great secret which God ever conceals from those who are wise in their
own conceits." As appears from the
Currus Triumphalis and other of his
works, he belonged to the religious order
of S. Benedict, and he is said to have
been canon of the priory of S. Peter in

---

* See Basil Valentine's treatise, entitled "Practica,
with the Twelve Keys and an Appendix," p. 313 of *The
Hermetic Museum Restored and Enlarged*, Vol. I., London,
4to, 1893.

Erfurt. It is further stated that his philosophical "Last Testament" remained concealed for a number of years in the high altar of the church belonging to the priory. There seems, at first sight, no reason to challenge the literal veracity of these matters ; the conventual institutions of the middle ages were frequently centres of scientific research ; innumerable monks have practised alchemy ; and works which their authors regarded as too good for the time when they were written, have been entombed for the benefit of a more deserving epoch both before and after the age of Basil Valentine. There is some occasion, notwithstanding, for suspecting that here, as in everything connected with the alchemists, the most simple facts are apparently the most deceptive. " Even unto the points and pricks here are to be found great mysteries." The suspicion is not the result of an over great subtlety on the part of modern mystical criticism, which is accused, and not always unjustly, of everywhere supposing the

wonderful ; it was far back in the early
seventeenth century that the doubt was
raised originally, and such investigations
as were possible have tended rather to
confirm than dispose of it. It is advanced that the monastic character
assumed by Basil Valentine was simply
a veil and an evasion to conceal his real
identity, and, further, that his name was
a pseudonym which was Hermetic and
allegorical in its significance. Maximilian Stoel, the author of a handbook
of practical medicine, which is now most
readily accessible in its fourth edition,
adopted this view.* So also did
Boerhaave, the celebrated physician of
Leyden, whose proposed chronological
history of the alchemists has been a loss
yet to be repaired.† Jacobus Tollius
contrived to resolve the enigma of the

---

* See *La Médicine Pratique*, forming the seventh
division of the *Encyclopédie des Sciences Médicales*, Paris,
1834, 8vo.

† On this and other points consult Dallowe's translation
of Boerhaave's *Elements of Chemistry*, 2 vols., 1735, 4to ;
also Herman Boerhaave : His Academical Lectures on
Lues Venerea, translated, London, 1763, 8vo.

assumed name by a consideration of the philosophical significance attaching to the two words in Greek and Latin respectively.* According to this interpretation, Basil in Greek is equivalent to royal, while Valentine is the Latin *valendo*. The union of the two terms formulates the symbol of power "which gives the regulus for the penetration of bodies." In another aspect, Basil Valentine signifies "the mighty king," who rules by initiation and adeptship "the three analogical worlds of occult philosophy." This interpretation of itself has little but a show of ingenuity to recommend it, yet as early as the year 1515 the identity of Basil Valentine was involved in so much uncertainty that the Emperor Maximilian the First, in his passion for the sciences, searched the Benedictine archives at Rome, and also made many inquiries in different monasteries about him, but without

---

* Jacobus Tollius : *Fortuita. In quibus præter critica nonulla, tota fabularis historia Græca Phœnicia Ægyptiaca chemiam pertinere asseritur.* Amsterdam, 1687, 8vo.

success. Vincent Placcius, one of the
earliest bibliographers and investigators
of the secret history of anonymous and
pseudonymous authors, affirms that the
real name of Valentine was Tholden.*
Others state that it was John Estchenreuter. The evidence for the statement
of Placcius is not satisfactory, and as
Prosper Marchand calls his curious work
mare magnum erratorum, it might be
unwise under any circumstances to accept
him as a guide. On the other hand,
the alternative statement, equally unsup-
ported by reference, appears in the
monographs of certain biographical dictionaries which are not very trustworthy,
if only because they betray little or no
acquaintance with the works of Basil
Valentine.

In order to appreciate the assertion
of Vincent Placcius, it must be noted
that it was owing to the solicitude of
John Tholden Hessius, that is, Johann
Thoelde, that the works of Basil Valen-

* *Theatrum Anonymorum et Pseudonymorum.* In two
parts. Hamburg, 1708, Fol.

tine began to be issued from the press. Under his editorial auspices *The Tract of the Great Stone* appeared in 1602, the treatise *Concerning Natural and Supernatural Things* in 1603, and *The Triumphal Chariot of Antimony* in 1604. That Placcius was aware of these facts seems doubtful, but he knew that in 1603 there was published at Eissleben a work entitled *Haligraphia*, on the title-page of which Thoelde is indicated as the author.* Now in 1644, under the auspices of another editor, a certain portion of this book was translated into Latin, and published as a work of Basil Valentine † under the slightly altered name of *Haliographia*. The claim of its editor that it is produced from the

---

* *Haligraphia :* that is, a Complete and Exhaustive Description of all the Mineral Salts, effectively describing the Salt of the First Matter, the tests for Salt Waters, the means of obtaining the Salt of the Sun through fire, by various methods, and the improvement of the same. By Johann Thoëlde Hesse. At the cost of Jacob Apel, bookseller, Eissleben, 1603, 8vo.

† It represents less than half the original, namely, from p. 168 onwards, as far as p. 310, missing the *Conclusio Autoris*, and other matter at the end.

manuscripts of the great alchemist seems wholly without foundation ; its attribution to Valentine may perhaps be accounted for by a blunder ; but there is no reason for supposing that it was other than an original storehouse of Hermetic theories and experiments, compiled by Thoelde himself. That so far as he is known at all he is known chiefly as the editor of Valentine does not preclude Thoelde from having appeared independently as an author, and so early as the year 1599 we find that he actually did so.* At the same time, it is possible for a mistake to have arisen through a misconception of some prefatory verses prefixed to the first *Haligraphia.*

Sic tu Mater es autorum, quos, Tholde,
    sophorum,
Eruis e tenebris, dasque videre diem.
Per te Basilius lucem squallore remoto,
    Cernit, Basilii mater es alma tui.*

---

* Information concerning the Revolting Malady called Red Dysentery, Diarrhea, and the extremely swift and dangerous sickness of the Pestilence. By Johann Tholden Hesse. Erfurt, 1599, 4to (a pamphlet of 22 pages).

* From the prefatory verses of Hermannus Kircnerus.

And again :—

Depromis Sal, Tholde, penu mortalibus ; ergo
  Condimenta coquus, tumque Hygiea paret
Non condus sis, Basilii monumenta recondens,
  Sed promus, pateat Basiliique penu.
Quo mage Basilii a doctis nunc scripta
  leguntur,
  Tanto major erit gloria, Tholde, tua.*

But the reference was not to the *Haligraphia*, but to Thoelde's editorial labours over Basil Valentine, then in progress, and probably well known to his friends.

While, however, there is no reason for fathering the *Haligraphia* upon Valentine, with Thoelde as editor, so is there less ground for identifying Thoelde with Valentine, or Valentine with any of his family, which is the course that is countenanced by Placcius on the authority of a vague reference.

The claim of John Estchenreuter to have worn the mask of Basil Valentine, is negatively more difficult to dis-

---

* From the prefatory verses of M. Johannes Tanckius, who himself shortly afterwards figured as an editor of alchemical literature.

pose of, because nothing is known about him, nor, indeed, has it been possible to discover by whom his claim has been preferred. At the period of Theolde's activity, we find Johannes Tanckius editing a collection of alchemical tracts, among which there is a brief epistle by Gallus Eschenreuter, or Schonreuter, but there is nothing known concerning him. *

Boerhaave denies that there was a monastery of S. Peter's at Erfurt, but on this point there is no reasonable doubt. A certain Mollenbæck,—whose identity is difficult to determine, while his record does not seem to remain, so far, at least, as libraries in England are concerned—is said to have visited it personally, and to have ascertained from the prior that the name of Basil Valentine did not appear on the records. What is more to the purpose is the testimony of Joannes Mauritius Gudenus, the historian of

---

* See the Epistle of Gallus Schonreuter, Doctor of Medicine and Ordinary Physical Chemist at Galenstadt, addressed to William Gratalorum. It is the third tract in the collection, entitled *Opuscula Chemica.* 1605, 8vo.

Erfurt, which is conclusive as to the existence of the convent, and testifies to the connection of the Alchemist therewith ; though the latter point is perhaps on the authority of the Alchemist, and not on that of the records of the place. *

It is obvious, of course, that if the name of Basil Valentine was assumed, he might still have been a monk of the convent, and he would have appeared in its archives only under his true title.

Despite the doubts that have been raised, the preponderating feeling of critics inclines to the belief that a person named Basil Valentine really existed, and actually filled that position in the devout life which is described in the *Currus Triumphalis.* This, however, is the utmost extent of their unanimity,

---

* " *Dicitur fuisse adeptus,*" says Gudenus, and again " *Eadem ætale (Scilicet,* 1413), *Basilius Valentinus in divi Petri monasterio vixit, arte medica et naturalium indagine mirabilis. Insuper iis accensetur quos in augmentum spei nominant aurum conjecisse, sic aliena dementia post secula fallit, ideo minima culpabilis, quod non nisi decipi amantes facultatibus exuat. Volumen Primum Rerum Moguntiacarum,* 1722. Fol. The history was published at Erfurt.

for, on the one hand it is asserted that
he was born at Alsace, on the borders
of the Rhine, and, on the other, that he
was himself a native of Erfurt. By
some again he is referred to the twelfth
century, and by others to the fourteenth ; the year 1394 has been named
as the date of his birth, and in 1415 he
is supposed to have commenced his
literary labours in Alchemy and
Hermetic Medicine. But these dates
are unable to support any test of
examination. A passage on page 181
of the present volume is conclusive as to
the earliest period. " You should know
that Antimony is used for a good many
purposes besides those of the typographer." It is perhaps difficult to
assign the exact date when Antimony
was first used as an alloy for the
founding of metal types, but the close of
the fifteenth century is likely to have
been the earliest period. There is, however, another and more important point.
The reader of the *Currus Triumphalis*
will find numerous references therein to

the recent appearance in Germany of the venereal scourge, which he calls the French disease—*Morbus Gallicus* and *Lues Gallica.* Now it appears to be certain, from abundant historical testimony, that the name of *Morbus Gallicus* was given to the complaint after the expedition of the French, under Charles VIII., to Naples, which took place in 1495. *

Basil Valentine is one of the few Alchemical writers who does not, at least in the undoubtedly genuine works, such as the *Currus Triumphalis* and the

---

* A synopsis of the testimony is as follows : In 1497, Nicolaus Leonicenus, of Vicentia, calls it by this name, though he denies the novelty of the disease, saying : "I can by no means imagine, with some, that this complaint never appeared till now." In 1498, Natalis Montesaurus, of Verona, remarks upon "those dispositions commonly called *Mal Franzozo.*" In 1499, the Spaniard, Gaspar Torella, narrates that the disease broke out in Alvernia in the year 1493, thence making its way into Spain, afterwards into Italy, and from Italy into all Europe. Joannes de Vigo, of Genoa, writing in 1503, says that it appeared almost all over Italy in the month of December, 1494, and he adds : "The French disease, when once it comes to be confirmed, seldom admits of any other than a palliative cure." Leonardus Schmai, of Salzburg, in 1518, bears witness to the same date, and makes use of the same name. In the year following,

Twelve Keys, betray the approximate date of his treatise by citations from slightly anterior adepts. On the whole, it is safe to place him at the end of the fifteenth and the beginning of the sixteenth centuries. He had probably passed the prime of life when he entered upon his labours in literature, and a whole century was destined to elapse before any of his works found their way into the hands of the printer. The following bibliographical list, while it includes all his extant treatises, in the matter of the dates appended does not

---

1519, Ulrichus de Hutten, a German, discoursed upon a "method of curing the French disease by Guaiacum," fixing 1493 for the date, and Naples for the place of its appearance. Joannes Baptista Montanus, 1550, affirms, on the other hand, that it was the soldiers of Columbus who imported the disease from Antigua, and the West India Islands, to the siege of Naples, in 1496. In 1554, Joannes Langius, of Limburg, speaks of the French disease, maintaining that "although some would have it to be a new one," it is "no other than a farrago of diseases known to the ancients." Compare also Bernardinus Tomitanrus, of Padua, 1566 ; Joannes Astruc, *De Morbis Veneris :* Adrianus Tollius : Herman Boerhaave, etc. See further, John Armstrong's "Synopsis of the History and Cure of Venereal Diseases," London, 1737, 8vo.

necessarily determine the original period of publication in every case.

Concerning Natural and Supernatural Things : also concerning the First Tincture, Root, and Spirit of Metals : how they are generated, brought forth, smelted, altered, and augmented. A true account, by Frater Basil Valentine, of the Benedictine Order, printed from his own manuscript by John Tholden Hessius, *cum privilegio.* Leipzig, at the cost of Jacob Apel, bookseller. A.D., 1603.

Frater Basil Valentine's Treatise concerning the Great Stone of the Ancients, whereat so many thousands of Masters have worked since the beginning of the world. Accompanied by his clear repetition and reiteration, wherein the true Light of the Wise is philosophically exhibited. Together with an account of the principal metals and their properties. II. Of the Microcosmos, or the small world of man. III. Of the Great Secret of the World, and

of the Medicine pertaining to man :
highly useful for all who desire to
know the source of wisdom. (This
tract is termed in some later editions
De Macrocosmo.) IV. Of the knowledge and hidden secrets of the
planets. Newly printed and published for the Sons of the Doctrine,
with appropriate diagrams, by John
Tholden Hessius, at the cost of
Jacob Apel, bookseller, in the year
1602.

The Revelation of Frater Basil Valentine, of the Benedictine Order,
concerning the Hidden Operations
directed towards the Universal
Subject. Also conclusions and
arguments from all his writings and
treatises on Sulphur, Vitriol, the
Magnet Stone, both the philosophical, from which the universal
originates, and the ordinary, which
originates the particular. (The first
treatise in this volume is better
known under the Latin title, *Apoca-
lypsis Chemica.*) Printed at the

expense of John Birkner, bookseller in Erfurt, 1624.

Frater Basilius Valentinus, of the Benedictine Order : Twelve Keys, whereby the doors are opened to the Ancient Stone of our Forefathers, and wherein the inexhaustible fountains of all health are found. Frankfort, 1611. (A Latin translation stands first in the Golden Tripod of the celebrated Michael Maier. Other editions in German appeared in 1677, 1700, and 1717.)

Azoth ; or, the secret Aureliæ of the Philosophers, faithfully and clearly explaining the First Matter, and the famous Stone of the Philosophers, unto the sons of Hermes, by way of a Philosophical Enigma, parabolic colloquy, the Smaragdine Table of Hermes, and the Saturnian Parables and Figures of Frater Basil Valentine. Interpreted by M. Georgius Beatus. Frankfort, 1613. (A French translation of this work appeared at Paris in 1624. It is difficult to say

how much, if any, of the original is
to be attributed to Valentine.)

Haliographia: concerning the Preparation, the Use, and the Virtues of all
Salts, mineral, animal, and vegetable;
from the manuscripts of Basilius
Valentinus, collected by And. Sal-
minicius, Bononia, 1644, 8vo.
(Doubtful.)

Secret Books, or Last Testament of
Basil Valentine, of the Benedictine
Order. Copied from the original
which was discovered in the high
altar of the Church at Erfurt, under
a marble tablet. Now printed in
accordance with numerous requests
on the part of the Sons of the
Doctrine. Strasburg, at the cost of
Caspar Dietzel, 1645.* (Contains
long treatises on mines and the

---

* "According to Olaus Borrichius, he enclosed his
writings in one of the pillars of the abbey church; they
remained for many years in this hiding-place, but were at
length discovered by the fortunate violence of a thunder-
bolt."—*Lives of Alchemystical Philosophers.* But Olaus
Borrichius wrote his *De Arte et Progressu Chemiæ* in 1668,
and probably derived his information from the so-called
Last Testament.

generation of metals, a commentary on The Twelve Keys, and other matters, but it is in all probability spurious.)

The Fifth Part of the Last Testament of that estimable Hermetic Philosopher, Frater Basil Valentine; part of which has never been previously printed, part of which is now published in completely fresh order, and differs from former exemplars. All translated literally from a secret manuscript, printed for the public good, by John Hiskias Cardilucius,. Com. Pal., Phil., et Med., etc. (Apparently a spurious *réchauffé*.)

In addition to these there is the *Manifestatio Artificiorum*, Erfurt, 1624, 8vo, which the present editor has not been able to trace, except in its French edition, published in 1646, under the title *Révélation des Mystères des Teintures essentielles des sept Métaux, et de leur Vertus Medicinales.* There is also a *Manuductio Medicinæ* mentioned by Boerhaave, and by no other writer. Finally, there is the "Triumphal Chariot of Antimony," which is translated in the following pages; this is by far the most important, as it is also the most lucid and simple, of all Valentine's works; it has done more than any other to establish his reputation as a chemist on the solid basis of plain, practical experiment. It is not, therefore, surprising that it achieved an immense success, that it has passed through . many editions, and has been translated into various languages, while it is still a subject of reference for the archæology of exoteric chemistry. Its presentation in accessible form to the modern student of the old alchemists will, it is believed, prove of good service in redeeming those profound investigators of Nature from the undeserved disdain of to-day, albeit Basil Valentine himself stands scarcely in need of vindication, for even the biographical dictionaries * of the

---

* "Among his discoveries, since improved on, and still medical preparations in constant use, are sulphuric ether, vinegar from honey-water, sugar of lead, litharge, fulmi-

early nineteenth century did honour to the philosopher of Erfurt. At the same time, there will be some satisfaction in citing the panegyric of a French scientist, Louis Figuier.

" Every one," says the author of *L'Alchimie et les Alchimistes*, " is acquainted with the remarkable discoveries relative to Antimony which are contained in the celebrated work of Basil Valentine, *Currus Triumphalis Antimonii.* The German Alchemist had so thoroughly investigated the properties of this metal, scarcely indicated before him, that we find many facts stated in his treatise which in our day have been brought forward as modern discoveries. In the same work Basil Valentine specifies many other chemical preparations of the first importance, such as spirit of salt, or our hydro-chloric acid, derived after our own manner from marine salt and oil of vitriol (sulphuric acid). He

---

nating gold, many mercurial preparations. empyreumatic carbonate of ammonia, claimed as his own by Sylvius Deleboe, etc."—*Biographie Universelle.*

gives the method of obtaining brandy
by the distillation of wine and. beer,
rectifying the product of the distillation
on calcined tartar (carbonate of potass).
He even teaches the extraction of copper
from its pyrites (sulphur), by first of all
transforming it into vitriol of copper
(sulphate of copper), with the help of
moist air, and afterwards plunging a bar
of iron into the aqueous dissolution of
this product. This operation, which Basil
Valentine was the first to describe, was
often profitably made use of by Alchemists at a later date, but, notwithstanding
the fact of the precipitation of metallic
copper, they mistook it for a transmutation of iron into copper, or at least as
the commencement of a transmutation
which could be perfected by art. . . .
One may regard this Alchemist as
having been the first to obtain sulphuric ether, which he prepared by
distilling a mixture of spirit of wine
and oil of vitriol. In a word, there
are few chemical preparations known
to his period concerning which Basil

Valentine has not registered some valuable facts."

Concerning the subject matter of the "*Triumphal Chariot,*" it will be seen by the general reader, who has an elementary acquaintance with the properties of Antimony, that the account of Basil Valentine is correct, not only as to general characteristics, but in many points of detail. As to the value of the metal as a factor in the act of transmutation, the modern chemist is not in a position to adjudicate, nor have we as yet a canon of interpretation by which we can distinguish the true meaning of the adept.

The method of the translation which follows is literal as regards all that is of practical importance ; for the rest, while it is by no means, and in no sense, an abridgment, it makes for brevity by the skilful compression of a prolix and tautological original. The translation has been subjected to revision at the hands of the editor, and the general plan, it is believed, will commend itself not only to the English reader, but to those who are acquainted with the *Currus Triumphalis* in either its German or Latin guise.

In conclusion, it may be added that no particulars are forthcoming as to Theodore Kerckringius, the commentator, who is interesting by his aspirations and his modesty. He does not appear to have entered a second time into the field of Hermetic literature. In the year 1670 he published, at Amsterdam, a century of anatomical observations, under the title *Spicilegium Anatomicum*, a very beautiful specimen of typography, adorned with valuable plates, but having no connection with esoteric medicine or chemistry.

ARTHUR EDWARD WAITE.

TO THE ILLUSTRIOUS,

VENERABLE, SAINTLY, AND BLESSED

MEN,

ADEPTS OF THE TRUE PHILOSOPHY,

LOVERS OF VIRTUE,

LORDS OF FORTUNE,

DESPISERS OF THE WORLD,

WHOSE LIFE IS HOLINESS IN HOLINESS,

KNOWLEDGE IN KNOWLEDGE,

AND WHOSE WORK CONSISTS IN THE

RELIEVING OF THE SICK

AND POOR.

B

DEDICATORY EPISTLE.

I T is not arrogance, but reverence, saintly and blessed men, that emboldens me to address you, whom I do not know, but whom I admire, love, venerate, and all but worship. For, though you are strangers to me, I know what sort of men you are, and what you have attained ; so that even if you were known to me, I would address you rather as Alchemists, than by your own proper names. In return for this dedication I expect no reward but to bask in the rays of your favour, and to be promoted in the way you know, since you will see from this book that I am in the straight road, and am mounting to the bright temple of knowledge by the right path. Do not refuse me the kindness which I here publicly confer on the lovers of Alchemy, which also, the inventor Apollo and lord Mercury do not forbid me to shew forth, since, in the words of Basilius, I have already gained a place in a higher class. To speak to you in your own phraseology, Mercury appeared to me in a dream, and brought me back from my devious courses to the one way. " Behold me clad not in the garb of the vulgar, but in the philosopher's mantle!" —so he said, and straightway began to leap along the road in headlong bounds. Then, when he was tired, he sat down, and, turning to me, who had followed him in the spirit, bade me mark that he no longer possessed that youthful vigour with which he would at the first have overcome every obstacle, if he had not been allowed a free course. Encouraged by his friendly salutation, I addressed him in the following terms : " Mercury, eloquent Scion of Atlas, and father of all Alchemists, since thou hast guided me hitherto, shew me, I pray thee, the way to those Blessed Isles, which thou hast promised to reveal to all thine elect children." " Dost thou remember," he

replied, "that when I quitted thy laboratory, I left behind me a garment so
thoroughly saturated with my own blood,
that neither the wind could efface it, nor
all-devouring time destroy its indelible
essence? Fetch it hither to me, that I
may not catch a chill from the state of
perspiration in which I now am; but let
me clothe myself warmly in it, and be
closely united thereto, so that I may
safely reach my bride, who is sick with
love. She has meekly borne many
wrongs, being driven through water and
fire, and compelled to ascend and descend
times without number—yet has she been
carried through it all by the hope of
entering with me the bridal chamber,
wherein we expect to beget a son
adorned from his birth with the royal
crown which he may not share with
others. Yet may he bring his friends to
the palace, where sits enthroned the
King of Kings, who communicates his
dignity readily and liberally to all that
approach him." I brought him the garment, and it fitted him so closely, that it

looked like an iron skin securing him
against all the assaults of Vulcan. "Let
us proceed," he then said, and straightway sped across the open field, while I
boldly strove to keep up with my guide.
Thus we reached his bride, whose virtue
and constancy were equal to his own.
There I beheld their marvellous conjugal
union and nuptial consummation, whence
was born the son crowned with the royal
diadem.   When I was about to salute
him as the King of Kings and Lord of
Lords, my Genius stood by me, and
warned me not to be deceived, since this
was only the King's forerunner, but not
the King himself whom I sought. When
I heard the admonition, I did not know
whether to be sad or joyful.   "Depart,"
then said Mercury, "with this bridal
gift, and when you come to those disciples who have seen the Lord himself,
shew them this sign"—and therewith he
gave me a gold ring from his son's
finger.   "They know the golden branch
which must be consecrated to Proserpina
before you can enter the palace of Pluto.

When he sees this ring, perhaps one will open to you with a word the door of that chamber, where sits enthroned in his magnificence the Desire of all Nations, who is known only to the Sages."' When he had thus spoken, the vision vanished, but the bridal gift that I still held in my hand, shewed me that it had not been a mere dream. It was of gold, but to me more precious than the most prized of all metals. Unto you I will shew it when I am permitted to see your faces, and to converse with you freely. Till that earnestly wished-for time, I bid you farewell. When I behold you, the sight will be to me more pleasant by far than that of Mercury, or my Genius. I, your humble servant and worshipper, shall easily recognize you by your auroral necks and ambrosial locks, which do give forth a fragrant odour.

To the Reader.

I WISH to deal candidly with you, gentle reader, and I therefore present to you here the work of Basil Valentine in a Latin garb, in order that it may be widely understood, with a Commentary of my own. To me he spoke in German, and without a commentator; I studied his work carefully, because I believed his promises, practically carried out all his directions, yet incurred much useless expense, made many mistakes, and, though I went through each operation more than ten times, could not succeed, not through the Author's, but, as I will confess honestly, through my own fault. For Basil is the Prince of all chemists, and the most learned, upright, and lucid of all alchemistic writers. He tells the careful student everything that can be known in Alchemy : of this I can

most positively assure you, not as though
I had already attained, or knew everything ; that would be a bold assertion.
But what I have already learned from
this writer fills me with hope, the aliment
of the Alchemist, that I shall attain the
remainder also. The Author needs no
further commendation ; did I add more
it would be insufficient to satisfy those
who reject this. The Commentary
which I subjoin, I do not commend. In
these notes I only give information which
in itself is humble enough, but the want
of which has cost me many thousands.
If you do not care to avoid this expense,
you may do without my guidance. You
will learn perhaps through your own
mistakes, if neither money nor patience
fail you. My guides have been constant
attention and the most careful thought ;
nor do you need any other leaders. So
therefore do without me, by all means,
if you can afford it. But if you wish to
avoid unnecessary delay, mistakes, and
useless expense, I may be to you a not
quite worthless counsellor, or at least a

humble finger-post, when perchance you stand perplexed by the multiplicity of intersecting roads. Farewell! If you will take my advice, reject not my services, and you will enjoy many advantages. Again farewell!

The Triumphal Chariot of Antimony,

BY

Basilius Valentinus,

WITH

The Commentary of

Theodore Kerckringius,

A Doctor of Medicine.

————

WHEREAS I, Basil Valentine, belong to the religious order of S. Benedict, and such a life requires a higher spirit of holiness than that which satisfies the multitude in this profane age, I consider it my duty to declare at the outset that it is necessary for the disciple of the Spagyric Art to know how he should lay stable foundations, so that his structure may not be at the mercy of the winds, or be shaken into ruins by every stormy gust. In dealing thus thoroughly with my subject, I am thinking not only of the present age, but of future generations, when we shall be in our graves, and when of our contemporaries, neither king nor peasant will be surviving. This object I pursue not only for the honour and glory of the Divine Majesty, but also in order that men may render to God implicit obedience in all things.

I have found that in this Meditation there are five principal heads, which must be diligently considered, as much by all who are in possession of the wisdom of philosophy as by all who aspire after that wisdom which is attained in our art. The first is the invocation of God ; the second, the contemplation of Nature ; the third, true preparation ; the fourth, the way of using ; the fifth, the use and profit. He who does not carefully attend to these points will never be included among real Alchemists, or be numbered among the perfect professors of the Spagyric science. Therefore we will treat of them in their proper order as lucidly and succinctly as we can, in order that the careful and studious operator may be enabled to perform our Magistery in the right way.

First, there should be the invocation of God, flowing from the depth of a pure and sincere heart, and a conscience which should be free from all ambition, hypocrisy, and vice, as also from all cognate faults, such as arrogance, boldness, pride, luxury, worldly vanity, oppression of the poor, and similar iniquities, which should all be rooted up out of the heart —that when a man appears before the Throne of Grace, to regain the health of his body, he may come with a conscience weeded of all tares, and be changed into a pure temple of God, cleansed of all that defiles. For "God is not mocked," as worldly men fondly suppose; He is not mocked, I say, but will be called upon with reverence and fear, and acknowledged as the Creator of all, with proper proofs of obedience. For what has man that he does not owe to God?—whether you look at his body, or at the soul which works in his body. Does he not nourish the latter with the

word of His mercy? and has not he
promised to it eternal life? Does he
not give to our bodies food and clothing,
without which we could not even live?
All this man must obtain from the
Blessed Father, who has created the
earth, things visible and invisible, the
firmament, elements, vegetables, animals,
and all things. Hence a wicked man
can never obtain the true Medicine,
much less become partaker of the
heavenly eternal bread.

Therefore, let all your hope be
stayed on God, and let constant prayer,
to impart to you this Blessing, be the
beginning of your work, in order that
you may safely reach the end, for the
"fear of God is the beginning of wisdom."

He who would seek the greatest of
all earthly benedictions, the knowledge
of all created good, and of the effectual
virtue which God has liberally implanted
in stones, herbs, roots, seeds, animals,
plants, minerals, metals, and all things,
must fling away every earthly thought,

hope only for freedom of heart, and pray to God with the greatest humility. Thus, the aspiration after freedom will soon be realized. This truth no one will call in question who knows that it is God who redeems Israel from all foes, and not only Israel but all that call upon Him with a contrite and broken spirit.

The first head of our teaching, then, must be prayer, which we call the INVO-CATION OF GOD, and see that it comes not forth out of feigned lips, but is the fruit of faith and confidence, like that of the Centurion of Capernaum; in humility and contrition, like that of the Canaan-itish woman ; in charity, like that of the Samaritan who took up the wounded man on the way to Jericho, pouring into his wounds wine and oil, and paying his expenses at the inn, with an injunction that proper care should be taken of him ; in brief, let the prayer be offered up in that spirit of Christian charity which desires to share what it obtains with its neighbour ; then you will doubtless attain

the object of your undertaking, viz.,
riches and health.*

Next in order after prayer follows
CONTEMPLATION, by which we apprehend

---

* It is not for me to criticise by praise or blame what the
Author here says about piety, the worship of God, and the
invocation of His Name. No doubt it was natural for Basil
to write as he did, and my business does not extend beyond
the task of rendering his remarks in Latin. In the meantime, I have endeavoured to acquit myself of my task so as
to give as little offence as possible to more advanced thinkers.
The Scripture says that godliness is profitable to all things,
and prayer is the most important exercise of godliness. If
prayer fulfilled no other purpose, it would at least be useful
in imparting earnestness to every search, and concentrating
the mind on the object in view. It prevents all distraction,
and that perfunctory treatment of our problem which is one
of the most frequent causes of failure. It often happens in
this search that what you vainly endeavoured to understand
for many days, suddenly is rendered plain to you in a single
moment by an instantaneous flash of inspiration, which one
would be ungrateful not to attribute to Divine assistance.
But if your oration, or prayer, is to be of any avail, there
must also be co-operation on your part : the solution which
you then find, by dint of perseverance and concentrated effort,
may be fitly called revelation. This would never have come
to you without oration and co-operation ; and yet, as the
solution is nowhere contained in the process by which it is
sought, it appears to you like a marvel, and a celestial revelation. Thus, if prayer be the power of concentration, we can
easily understand how it is the means of placing temporal and
spiritual blessings within our reach. Hence prayer is highly
commended by Basil, and all the Sages ; for godliness is
profitable to all things, and especially to that which is the
greatest of all earthly blessings.

the essential properties of a thing, the circumstances by which it is conditioned, its matter, its form, its operations and their source, whence it is infused and implanted, how it is generated by the Stars, formed by the elements, produced and perfected by the three principles.

Again, it enables us to understand how the body of anything can be dissolved, *i.e.,* resolved into its first matter or essence; to this change I have referred in my other writings as the transmutation of the last substance into the first, and of the first substance into the last.*

This Contemplation, which forms the second part of our work, is heavenly, and spiritually apprehended, for only the spiritual mind can grasp the circum-

---

* Here you have an epitome of all the elaborate and obscure teaching of the Sages, which is comprised in so many books. The Author had a perfect knowledge of that spirit which permeates all creation, and is the efficient cause of all things, yet is everywhere bound up with the defile-ments and dross of matter; if freed from this dross, it returns to the purity of its substance, in which it produces every-thing, and becomes everything in every form. To comment on it, or attempt its explanation, would be trying to con-dense the work of all the Sages into the compass of a foot-note.

C

stances and foundation of all things.
Now, this Contemplation is two-fold :
one is called impossible, the other
possible. The former consists in endless meditations, which can have no
result because their object is intangible.
Such problems are the Eternity of God,
the Sin against the Holy Ghost, the
infinite nature of the Godhead. They
are incomprehensible, and necessarily
baffle the finite enquirer.

The other part of Contemplation,
which is possible, is called *Theoria.* It
deals with the tangible and visible which
has a temporal form—shewing how it
can be dissolved and thereby perfected
into any given body; how every body
can impart the good or evil, medicine
or poison, which is latent in it; how
the wholesome is separated from the
unwholesome; how to set about des-
truction and demolition for the purpose
of really and truly severing the pure
from the impure without any sophistic
guile.

This separation is brought about by

different manual operations, and in various other ways, some of which are already familiar to the multitude, while others are by no means well known. They are as follows : CALCINATION, SUBLIMATION, REVERBERATION, CIRCULATION, PUTREFACTION, DIGESTION, DISTILLATION, COHOBATION, FIXATION, and the like. The meaning of these terms gradually comes to be understood by the practical experimentalist. In the same way you come to see the meaning of the terms : movable, fixed, white, red, black, blue, green, viz., by sound practical experience. For the operator may err, and deflect from the rectilineal way, but that Nature, when rightly treated, should ever err, is impossible.

If, therefore, the substance be not perfectly dissolved, and set free from all corporeal poison, know that you have made a mistake. Retrace your steps, learn the theory more perfectly, and enquire more accurately into the method of operation, so as to find the true foundation, and certainty in the separation of all things—which is a matter of the greatest importance.

This, then, is the second foundation of philosophy, and follows upon Invocation. It is the most important aspect of our Art, and is expressed in the following words : Seek first the Kingdom of God, and His justice— by Invocation—and all other things that men need, for the support and health of the body, will be added unto you.

On theory, which lays bare the most intimate relations of things, follows PREPARATION, which is perfected by manual operation, and yields a tangible result. Out of preparation arises knowledge, which lays bare the foundations of Medicine.

Manual Operation requires diligent application, and knowledge is founded on experience, while the difference between the two is set forth by Anatomy. Operation shews how all things spring into existence, and become visible. Knowledge points out practical methods, and is nothing but Confirmation; manual operation shewing the good, eliciting the latent and hidden nature, and bringing it forth into the light for good ; for as in spiritual things the way of the Lord must be prepared, so in this Art also the way must be opened and made straight, in order that the goal may be reached without any false step or aberration.*

After preparation, and especially after separation of good and bad (brought about by dissolution), we must proceed to the Proportions of Weight, or *dosis.* For you must avoid taking either too little or too much : this is a point to which the physician should pay the closest attention, if he would not "make a fat churchyard."†

When the Medicine is diffused

---

* In this third part, manual experiment is indispensably necessary, since without it the student is driven about by every passing wind like a rudderless ship. Concerning this, it is difficult to give directions in writing. One hour of practice teaches more than many pages of the most lucid written instructions.

† If you do not know the right quantity of a Medicine, it may produce an effect directly the opposite of that which

through the whole body, to counteract its defects we become acquainted with its USES. For it may happen that a Medicine properly prepared, and given in proper quantity, is, nevertheless, rather harmful than curative, in certain diseases ; and therefore we must discover the conditions under which alone it is likely to be beneficial.

In answering this question, you must observe whether the wound is internal or external—for the treatment is widely different in the two cases. Hence you must go to the root of every disease, and determine whether it can be cured by external remedies only, or whether it must be driven out by internal applications. For if its centre lie hid within, you want a medicine which will penetrate to the centre and restore it ;

you contemplate as desirable. To discover the doctrine of doses by experience is very risky, and yet this is the only method by which it has been found out. In this matter we may profit by the teaching of our predecessors, and withal be rather over timid than over bold. Still, when Antimony is properly prepared, it is as harmless as cassia or manna. But in the first stages of its preparation, where it retains much of its poisonous crudity, you ought to be very careful.

else all your healing efforts will be
fruitless.*

An external disease, admitting of
external treatment, cannot be driven
inward without fatal results. If, while a
tree is putting forth leaves and blossoms,
you were to drive the sap inward or
downward, you would not only obtain no
fruit, but probably blast, wither, and
destroy the entire growth.

There is a great difference, then,
between fresh wounds, inflicted with a
sword or dagger, or in some other way,
and old wounds which have an internal
origin. Fresh wounds can be perfectly
cured only by external remedies ; but in
the case of internal diseases the external
application of oils, plasters, ointments, and
balms will be of little avail. The inward
fountain of the disease, whence the
morbid humours flow to the outward

---

*What is here said, about internal and external diseases,
merits careful attention. If the Reader be wise, he will
understand that Basilius here speaks ironically, in order to
lead all scorners and ignorant persons astray. While others
yield to indignation at his method of instruction, the true
student will gather the fruit which hangs in clusters among
the thorns.

parts, must be dried up.   Then the flux
will cease, and the evil can be cured by
means of diet alone.

It does not require much skill to
heal a common fresh wound ; any boor
can do so with a little crude lard.   But
to stop all the symptoms, by drying
up the fountain of an internal wound,
tests to the utmost the physician's
cunning.

Come hither, then, ye that claim to
be doctors of both branches of Medicine,
healers of internal as well as of external
diseases : see whether you can make
your claim good ; ask yourselves, in the
sight of God, whether you really possess
this knowledge, or whether it belongs to
you as a mere formal title of honour.
For as great as is the distance between
heaven and earth, so great is the difference between the art of healing internal
and external diseases.   If your honour-
able title be the gift of God, the same
God will also follow it up with blessing,
success, and happiness ; but if your title
be a vain imagination of your own am-

bitious heart, all your attempts will fail ; your honour will be grievously sullied, and you will prepare for yourself the fire of hell, which can no more be put out than it can be explained in words. For Christ says to His disciples : "Ye call me Lord and Master, and ye do well." Whoever, therefore, takes to himself a title of honour, should be careful to see whether he does well, whether he does not arrogate to himself too much, more than he knows or has learned, which would be an abuse of the title. Who ever calls himself a Doctor of both branches of Medicine must be skilled alike in internal and external pathology ; he should also know anatomy, which teaches the constitution of the human body, and the part in which every disease originates and is localized. He must know the remedies which are applicable to the several varieties of disease, and the peculiar conditions of external wounds. Good God ! If an examination were held on these points, how many doctors of both branches of

Medicine would be compelled publicly to declare their ignorance!

Once upon a time Doctors of Medicine were content to cure external wounds, and looked upon this task as part of their duty; but now they leave it to ignorant and inexperienced beginners, who hardly know "how to drive a donkey out of a field." These persons style themselves masters in the art of healing wounds, and great Doctors; and I am ready to admit that they have a better claim to such title than you, illustrious surgeon, who do most impudently arrogate to yourself a false title, calling yourself a Doctor of both branches of Medicine.

What more would you have, my lord Doctor? What say you, O expert Surgeon? If I were to put to you some searching questions respecting the nature and cure of external wounds, I should find that there is in you about as much knowledge as there is in the brain of a cock on the title page of a child's spelling-book.

Hence I would thus advise men of all ranks, who are anxious to obtain knowledge: Demand first of your masters true teaching, which consists in preparation and the proportion of ingredients; then you will hold your title with honour, and give real help to your fellow-men; you will also have good reason to return thanks to the Creator out of an unfeigned heart.

Let every one seriously consider in his own mind what he should do, what he should leave undone, and whether his title belongs to him of right, or not. Whoever assumes a title should know its meaning, and whether he is justified in claiming it. A rational man must be able to assign a reason for everything, and when he smells a dung-heap of a very penetrating odour, he should be able to say why he calls it good dung, and also why a certain person who has partaken of fragrant and sweet-smelling food, gives it out in the shape of highly malodorous excrement. The answer is to be found in the conditions of natural putrefaction and corruption. The same thing is observable in the transmutations of all fragrant substances. Hence the Sage should enquire what an odour is, whence it derives its properties, and how those properties can be turned to good account. For the earth is nourished with stinking dung, and precious fruits are produced thereby. To account for this phenomenon there is a multiplicity of causes which it would take a whole book to explain, if we attempted to describe, even briefly, all natural mutations and generations. But digestion and putrefaction are the Master Keys of the process. Fire and air produce a kind of maturity, by which a change can take place out of water and earth. This is the kind of transmutation by which fragrant balsam becomes stinking dung, and stinking dung fragrant balsam. But you will ask me why I quote such simple and absurd examples. · The example, I confess, smacks of the stables rather than of the drawing-room ; but the careful student of Nature will understand me all the better for that reason. He will see that the highest things become the lowest, and the lowest are changed into the highest—*i.e.*, a medicine into a poison, and a poison into a medicine ; a sweet thing into a bitter, acid, and corrosive substance ; and a common thing, on the other hand, into something useful.

But, good God!—how difficult it is for us shortlived men to explore the whole compass of Nature. Thou hast reserved to Thyself many things in Creation which are objects of marvel rather than of knowledge. Therefore permit me to the end of my life to keep Thee in my heart, that in addition to the temporal health and wealth, which Thou givest freely, I may also obtain the salvation of my soul, and spiritual riches. Of this I dare not doubt, for Thou hast shed the balm and sulphur of my soul on the bitter cross—a balm which to the Devil is deadly poison, but to sinners the most potent medicine. I strive to heal the souls of my brethren with prayer, and their bodies with suitable remedies. May

God grant that we may all dwell together in His mansions on high!

But to return to the science of Antimony. You should know that all things contain operative and vital spirits, which derive their substance and nourishment from their bodies; nor are the elements themselves without these spirits, whether good or evil. Men and animals have within them an operative and vitalizing spirit, and if it forsakes them, nothing but a dead body is left. Herbs and trees have spirits of health, else no Art could turn them to medicinal uses. In the same way, minerals and metals possess vitalizing spirits, which constitute their whole strength and goodness: for what has no spirit has no life, or vitalizing power. Know that in Antimony also there is a spirit which is its strength, which also pervades it invisibly, as the magnetic property pervades the magnet.

Now, there are different kinds of spirits, which are partly visible, and yet cannot be touched as the natural body of a man can be touched. Such are especially those spirits which have fixed their domicile in the elements, spirits of fire, light, and other light-dispensing objects. Such are the aërial spirits which dwell in the air ; watery spirits in the water ; terrestrial spirits, or "earth men" in the earth, especially where there are rich veins of ore. These spirits have reason and sensation, are skilled in the different Arts, and can assume a variety of shapes, until the time of the judgment, which perhaps even now God has pronounced against them.*

Other spirits which cannot speak, nor exhibit themselves by their own power, are those which dwell in men and animals, in plants and minerals.

---

* What is here said about spirits looks like a medley from the works of some theologians who speak of intelligence being inherent in fire, air, and the other elements, and are ultimately doomed to eternal fire. The nature and the fate of these spirits we will leave to the omniscience and justice of God ; but as to the material spirits of Antimony, and other visible objects, all that our Author ascribes to them is true ; and the things they accomplish are far more wonderful than the fabulous achievements of any so-called supernatural beings.

They have an occult, operative life, and manifest themselves by the efficacy of their working ; when separated from bodies by our Art they have a most marvellous sanative virtue.

In this way the operative spirit and virtue of Antimony bestows its gifts, and imparts them to men, when it has been separated from its body so as to penetrate other bodies with its sanative virtue. In this process the Artist and Vulcan (fire) must be of one mind. The fire causes the separation, the Artist forms the substance. So the smith uses one fire and one material, viz., iron ; and yet produces out of them a great variety of different instruments, a spit, spurs, an axe, or some other tool. In the same way Antimony can be put to a great many different uses, wherein the smith is the skilled Artist, while the fire is, as it were, the key which opens, and practical experiment results in experience and a useful conclusion.

Alas, if men only had eyes to see, and ears to hear not merely what I say, but to understand the secret meaning, they would no longer drink those turbid and unwholesome potions, but would hasten hither, and receive the limpid water of the well of life!

It is my design to shew that those great doctors, who think themselves wise, are very fools, while my book may make many foolish and unlearned persons the depositaries of true wisdom.

All men who are real lovers of knowledge, and humbly seek after it by day and by night, are herewith cordially invited to listen to my teaching, to pore over my book with the greatest care, and thereby to obtain the desire of their hearts. Their gratitude will, after my death, raise me from the grave, and render my name immortal. If any one be opposed to my opinions, he will find a crushing reply in this work. Nor am I fearful that my disciples who, through my teaching, obtain the empire over Nature, will ever suffer my name to sink into oblivion, or to be bespattered with vile calumnies.

D

Know then, benevolent and sincere observer of art, that there are two kinds of Antimony, which differ widely from each other. One is beautiful, pure, and of a golden quality, containing a considerable amount of Mercury. The other has much Sulphur, is not so friendly to gold as the first, and is known by its beautiful, long, brilliantly white streaks. Now, one Antimony is more useful than the other, both for Alchemistic and Medicinal purposes. There are many different kinds of flesh, the flesh of fishes and the flesh of animals ; and as both are flesh, so two widely different substances may be called Antimony.

Many have written about the inward virtue of Antimony, but few know either the true foundation of its power, or the origin thereof. Their knowledge is verbal erudition only ; it is devoid of a solid grounding, and bears no fruit.

To write on Antimony, there is needed profound meditation, a large mind, a wide knowledge of its preparation, and of its true soul, in which consists all its usefulness. If you are familiar with these, you can truly tell what is good and medicinal, what is bad and poisonous, in it. It is surely worth while to enquire into the essential and fundamental nature of Antimony, and to discover how its venomous quality, against which so loud an outcry is raised, may be removed, and itself prepared, changed, and transmuted into a pure Medicine, containing not a single trace of poison.

Many Anatomists have subjected Antimony to all manner of singular torments and excruciating processes, which it is difficult either to believe or to describe. Their studies have led to no result, because they did not seek the true soul of Antimony, and, therefore, did not soon find that fictitious soul of which they were in search, their path being obscured with black colours which rendered invisible what they desired to see. Antimony, like Mercury, is comparable to a circle, without beginning or end, composed of all colours; and the more is always found in it, the more diligent and prudent the search which is made. One man's life is too short to discover all these mysteries. It is a most potent poison; then, again, it is free from poison, and a most excellent Medicine, both for external and internal application. This is hidden from many through their blindness, and they judge it to be a foolish, incredible, and vain thing. We must excuse them on account of their ignorance, and permit them to plead their stupidity in extenuation of their folly. The worst of it is that they will not be taught.

. Antimony has the four first qualities; it is frigid and humid, and yet hot and dry; it accommodates itself to the four seasons of the year, and is both volatile and fixed. Its volatility is poisonous, its fixed state free from all poison. Hence Antimony is one of the seven wonders of the world, and many have written about it without knowing the meaning of their own words; no one before me, and even

at the present time no one besides myself, has any real acquaintance with its
potency, virtues, powers, operation, and
efficacy.   If any such person could be
found, he would be worthy to be drawn
about in a triumphal car, like great
kings and warriors after mighty and
heroic achievements in the battlefield.
But I am afraid that not many of our
Doctors are in danger of being forcibly
placed in such a car.*

Men of this world, who are at the
same time students of our art, are so
given up to the desire of gain that they
can think only of the riches which Antimony is to bestow upon them ; they do
not realize that the medicinal virtues of
Antimony should be the first object of

---

* Read carefully all that our friend Basilius says in praise
of Antimony. You will find here no vain boasting or foolish
exaggeration, for as yet no man has been able to sound
the wonderful depths of this marvellous Medicine. We see
many things, new things are daily discovered, and still more
remain to be found out.   The resources of Antimony are as
inexhaustible and infinitely varied as those of fire, which are
not diminished by taking away from them.   Hence Basilius
rightly judged him who should sound the mystery of
Antimony worthy of a triumphal car.

our search, in order that the name of God shall be glorified, and that our fellowmen may be truly benefitted.

We admit that greater riches are to be found in Antimony than it is possible to imagine, even for me, though I know much more about this matter than you who are so exceedingly wise in your own conceits. But let none be afraid for this reason, or despair of ultimately attaining to this highest felicity of human life ; for the loving kindness of God is great in the dispensation of His gifts. But because of the ingratitude of men, He has covered their eyes, as it were, with cobwebs, so that they cannot perceive the mysteries hidden in this mineral form.

All clamour aloud : We want to be rich, rich ! Yes, you desire wealth, and say with Epicurus : Let us provide for our bodies, and leave our souls to take care of themselves. Even as Midas in the fable, you desire to change all things into gold. So are there numerous persons who seek this coveted wealth in Antimony, but since they do not care for

God, and have cast far away from them
the love of their neighbour, they will
look at the horse's teeth of Antimony for
ever without knowing anything about its
age or qualities. Like the wedding-
guests of Cana, they may behold the
miracle by which water is turned into
wine ; they may know that it was water,
and they may taste that now it is wine ;
yet they can never learn the way in
which the change was brought about.

Nevertheless, it is every one's duty
to investigate the mysteries and wonderful secrets which the Creator has infused
into all things. We may not be able to
understand and explain everything. Yet
many things are possible to industry and
perseverance ; and though many an one
may be severely handicapped in the
struggle for wealth and health, yet,
through the grace of God, he may still
attain thereto. Therefore he should not
think any labour too great which is likely
to advance his knowledge of Antimony.
Whoever, then, would perfectly understand the Anatomy of Antimony, should,

in the first place, become acquainted with the manner of its solution, so that he may be able to seize it in the right place, and proceed in the right way, without entering into devious paths. In the second place, he should learn how to regulate the fire, so that it shall be neither too fierce nor too feeble. Fire is the root of the whole matter. By means of fire the vitalizing spirits are extracted and dissolved for the purposes of our operation. But care must be taken not to mortify and destroy the spirit by means of too much heat.

The third point for consideration is the proportion of the substance, the discovery of the proper measure, as I have already noted, when enumerating the five points which are requisite in Alchemy. It is necessary to enlarge further upon this matter.

The substance is prepared by means of dissolution ; it is perfected by means of coction in fire. This is the axe that kills the ox, and divides it into parts. But men cannot partake of the flesh till it has been cooked over the fire, by which means the red colour of the meat is removed, and a white nutritious substance is substituted in its place. If a man, driven by hunger, were to eat the raw, red flesh, it would be a poison to him rather than a medicine, because the stomach has not sufficient natural heat to digest the raw material. In the same way, it will be so much the more dangerous for you to use Antimony before separation, preparation, and coction, as the mineral substance is more gross and poisonous in its raw state than that obtained from the animal body.

Therefore Antimony must be so thoroughly deprived of its poisonous nature that it can never again return to it, just as wine which has once been changed into vinegar by putrefaction and corruption, can never again produce the spirit of wine, but must always remain vinegar. But when, by means of distillation, the spirit alone is removed from the wine, so that the watery part is separated from the spirit, and the spirit is afterwards sublimed, the wine can never thenceforth become vinegar, even though it were kept a hundred years, but would always remain spirit of wine, just as the vinegar always remains vinegar.

This change of wine into vinegar is a wonderful thing, for thereby something is actually produced out of the wine which did not before exist in its vegetable essence. In the distillation of wine the first product is a spirit ; in the distillation of vinegar the first product is a watery substance, and thus a spirit, as I explained above. Hence the spirit of wine, being itself volatile, renders other things volatile, but the spirit of vinegar fixes and renders solid all medicaments, both mineral and vegetable, so that they attract fixed matter and expel fixed diseases.

Pay diligent attention to this fact, and observe it well, for here lies the master key of our whole Art.*

---

* Do not blindly believe these and similar assertions of Basilius, but keep your eyes wide open. Herein is the first key, herein the chief point of the whole Art. This will open

Antimony, which contains within itself its own vinegar, should be so prepared as to entirely remove its poisonous nature, in order that he who drinks it may not swallow with it any venom, but rather drive away and cast out all poison from his body.

The preparation of Antimony, or the Key of Antimony, is that by which it is dissolved, opened, divided, and separated. Such processes are calcination, reverberation, sublimation, as we have previously declared. In extracting its essence, in vitalizing its Mercury, the process is continued, and this Mercury must afterwards be precipitated in the form of a fixed powder. By our Art it can also become an oil, which is a specific against the new disease imported into this country by French soldiers.

---

to you the first portal and the last, leading to the chamber of the King. You now stand on the threshold of the work. If you take a false turning at this point, or enter by a wrong door, the whole of your subsequent journey will be misdirected. He who holds the right key in his hand, and has that strength to turn it which is supplied by Plutus (who is god of wealth), the entrance to the inmost shrine of Alchemy lies open before him.

The same process may be observed, for instance, in the brewing of beer ; barley, wheat, or other grain, must undergo all these processes before it becomes a palatable beverage. It must first be mashed and dissolved in water, as I have observed them do in Belgium and England, when I was a young man. This is Putrefaction, or Corruption. Then the water is poured off, and the moist grain is left in a warm place, till it germinates and sticks together. This is Digestion.

Thereupon the grains are once more separated from each other, and dried, either in the sun or before the fire. This is Reverberation and Coagulation.

The prepared germ is then ground in the mill. This is vegetable Calcination. It is afterwards cooked over the fire, and its nobler spirit is mingled with the water in a way which would not have been possible before it was so prepared. Thus, water becomes beer, and this we may call Distillation. If hops are added to the beer they are its vegetable salt, which preserves it from all adverse corrupting influences. This method of converting water into a fermented beverage by the extraction of the spirit of grain is unknown to the Spaniards and Italians, and in my native country of Germany I have only found a few, in the Rhenish districts, who understand such Art.

Afterwards a new separation takes place by means of Clarification. A little yeast is added to the beer, which stirs up its internal heat and motion, and thus, in time, the gross is separated from the subtle, and the pure from the impure. The beer thereby becomes a perfect beverage of great efficacy ; before this clarification this would not be, because such operative spirit was clogged and hindered by its own uncleanness from fulfilling its objects. Does not experience teach the same lesson in the case of wine ? It is not perfect, nor can it properly fulfil its object, till it has been freed from all impurity. Unclarified beer or wine is not half so intoxicating as beer or wine when it is purified.

After this, we may bring about another separation by means of Vegetable Sublimation. The spirit of wine, or beer, by this process, and by Distillation, is separated, and prepared in the form of another beverage, or ardent spirits. Here the operative virtue is separated from its body; the spirit is extracted by means of fire, and has deserted its inert and lifeless habitation, in which before it was domiciled.

If such ardent wine, or spirit of wine, be rectified, you have Exaltation. When this is done, the spirit of wine is several times distilled, and so condensed by being purified from all phlegm and wateriness that one measure is more effectual than twenty measures were before; it intoxicates more rapidly, and is volatile, and subtle in penetrating and acting upon substances.*

---

* Do not despise these remarks on the preparation of beer and wine. There may be apparent repetition here, but there is nothing superfluous. Return often mentally to this beershop; read, mark, learn, and inwardly digest all that is said. It may be that in this turbid water, which looks so unlikely, you may after all catch your fish. If the excess of

Here I exhort you, who desire through my teaching to secure health and riches as the reward of your study of Antimony, not to suppose that there is so much as a superfluous word or letter in what I have hitherto said. I tell you there are many words sprinkled up and down in my writings which may make it well worth your while to turn over the pages again and again, and to ponder very frequently the meaning of sentences in which every word is worth its weight in gold. Know that though the illustrations which I have given have a rustic and simple appearance, they set forth a grand truth of the highest moment. But it is neither desirable nor necessary to praise my own works : they will praise themselves, as soon as the suggestions contained in them are practically tried. I purposely use rude and common illustrations. For it is my business to set forth the hidden virtues of Antimony ;

---

light which prevails here should not enable you to see, no amount of obscure alchemistic reading will disperse your inward darkness.

and as this is a very profound and
abstruse speculation, it is useful to prepare the way by throwing upon my
subject all the light which can be gained
from common and familiar things ; otherwise, you might be in danger of losing
your road at the very outset of your
journey. Antimony is also likened to a
bird which is borne through the air on
the wings of the wind, and turns whither
it will. The wind, or air, here represents the Artist, who can move and
impel Antimony whither it pleases him,
and place it wherever he likes. He can
colour it red or yellow, white or black,
according to the way in which he regu-
lates the fire, since Antimony, like
Mercury, contains within itself all colours.

If a book be placed before an
illiterate person, he does not know what
the letters mean ; he stands staring
stupidly at the characters, like a cow at
a new gate. But if that person were
taught to read, were shewn the significa-
tion of the letters, and instructed in the
meaning of the work, he would no longer

be a prey to stupid wonder, but the why
and the wherefore of the whole thing
would be plain and familiar to him.
Such a book is Antimony to those who
have not yet learned to read it : hence
all such persons should pay the most
careful attention to my preliminary instruction, and should not be offended if I
offer to teach them the alphabet of Antimony. Let them study this alphabet
diligently, in order that they may learn
to read the book, and thus advance from
class to class in this our school of
Alchemy, until they have reached the
highest grade of all.

But at this point I remember that
there is, from time to time, a great
clamour, and cry of "Away with them,
crucify them, crucify them!" raised
against those who prepare medicines out
of poisons such as Mercury, Arsenic,
and Antimony. It is averred that by
means of such medicines many have met
with a sudden death, or are dragging on
a miserable existence. This clamour is
most persistently raised by those Doctors

E

of Medicine (save the mark!) who do not know the difference between a poison and a theriac, nor yet how a poison shall be prepared in order that it may become a salutary medicine, and exchange its malignancy for health-giving qualities. I protest against being numbered amongst the persons who administer to their patients orpiment, arsenic, and mercury, which, in their unprepared state, are, of course, deadly poisons.* But after legitimate preparation all venom is removed and expelled, and there remains only a Medicine which resists all internal poisons, and radically removes them. It is also the surest antidote against every unprepared poison, and

---

*At the time when Basilius wrote, the ignorance of certain physicians was so great that they administered as medicines many poisons in their raw and unpurified state, and ignorantly proscribed the means by which the Alchemists rendered them truly salutary to the human system. Against these pseudo-doctors honest Basilius and his friends were wont to inveigh with the greatest sharpness. But in this imperfect world truth is not necessarily victorious, and though the Alchemists had the better cause, their opponents had the advantage of numbers. Yet, even then, Paracelsus foresaw the dawn of better times which should be ushered in by the coming of the Artist Elias.

changes all such into its own wholesome nature.

This assertion will excite a fierce controversy among Doctors, and many will be ready to maintain to the last breath that it is utterly impossible to remove the deadly nature of mineral poisons. I do not wonder at their incredulity, since they are hopelessly ignorant of all similar preparations, and have no conception of the deeper mysteries of science. Yet those who are more reasonable will be ready to admit that it is possible considerably to improve a vile and worthless substance.

Moreover, you Doctors yourselves must admit that your object is to make better that bad thing which causes the disease. Must you not also acknowledge that the diseases of minerals, and especially of medicinal minerals, can be so removed that a state of perfect health may be restored, and that the medicines must thereby be rendered infinitely more efficacious. But I do not expect you to agree with me, since you are not

familiar with the method of preparation.
The unreasoning clamour of the majority:
" Poison, poison!" will doubtless carry
the day, just as the senseless clamour
of the Jews, " Crucify, crucify Him!"
doomed to death the Saviour of the
world, Whom the multitude pronounced
a most deadly and injurious poison,
while in reality He was the only true,
noble, and effectual Medicine of our
souls, come to deliver us from eternal
death, hell, the power of Satan, and all
other evils and misfortunes. This profound truth those supercilious Scribes
and Pharisees could and would not
understand, yet it was the truth then,
and will remain so throughout all eternity; nor will the devil, or death, or the
gates of hell, ever be able to prevail
against it, or to prove it a lie.

So I know that in spite of the
clamorous outcry raised against it by
quacks, mountebanks, and idle Doctors
resident in towns, yea, by all men who
profess to have any knowledge of the
noble Art which they disgrace, Antimony

will triumph and trample underfoot the
whole rout of its assailants, and its false
and hypocritical judges will receive the
same condemnation as the wicked Jews.
What a poor figure do they cut in my
eyes—all these grand, conceited magnificoes who solemnly admonish Emperors,
Kings, Princes not even to touch such
medicines with their lips, because they
are poisonous, noxious, and most dangerous. I will not attempt to refute them,
for they speak at random without the
slightest knowledge of their subject. I
will only say this, that I offer to give to
one who has swallowed the most deadly
of all poisons so powerful an antidote,
that, if he be left altogether to my treatment, the venom will at once be totally
expelled from his system.

As to the rest, I do not care in the
least whether you, Sir Doctor, who know
nothing at all about this matter, and
have never given the least thought to it,
condemn my medicine, or not ; it is
enough for me that I can prove its
efficacy, that I have prepared this Medi-

cine with my own hands, and administered it with unvarying success to great
numbers of people, who are ready to
bear me witness under their own hand
and seal.

If I ever had to dispute in the
schools with this quality of Doctor, who
cannot prepare his own medicines (such
as they are), but must leave that work to
another, I should justly claim pre-emi-
nence over him. For he does not even
know the colour of the remedies which
he prescribes. He has not the slightest
idea whether they are white or black, red
or grey, blue or yellow, or whether the
medicament is hot, cold, dry, or humid.
He only knows one thing—that he has
found the name of that medicine in his
books, and, pluming himself on the
antiquity of his hoary ignorance, he
claims the right of prior possession.

Here again I am tempted to cry
woe upon these foolish doctors whose
consciences are seared with a hot iron,
who do not care in the least for their
patients, and will be called to a terrible

account for their criminal folly on the day of judgment. Then they will behold Him Whom they have pierced by neglecting their neighbour's welfare, while pocketing his money, and they will see at last that they ought to have laboured night and day, in order to acquire greater skill in the healing of disease. Instead of this they complacently go on trusting to chance, prescribing the first medicine they happen to find in their books, and leaving the patient and the disease to fight it out as best they can. They do not even trouble to enquire in what way the medicines they prescribe are prepared. Their laboratory, their furnace, their drugs, are at the Apothecary's, to whom they rarely or never go. They inscribe upon a sheet of paper, under that magic word "*Recipe*," the names of certain medicines, whereupon the Apothecary's assistant takes his mortar, and pounds out of the wretched patient whatever health may still be left in him.

Change these evil times, oh God! Cut down these trees, lest they grow up

to the sky! Overthrow these over-
weening giants, lest they pile mountain
upon mountain, and attempt to storm
heaven! Protect the conscientious few
who quietly strive to discover the mysteries of Thy creation!

I will ask all my brothers in our
Monastery to unite with me in earnest
prayer, by day and by night, that God
may enlighten the ignorance of these
Pseudo-Doctors, that they may understand the virtues which He has implanted
in created things, and may learn also
that they can become manifest and
operative only by means of that preparation which removes all harmful and
poisonous impurities. I trust that God
will answer our prayer, and that some of
my brothers at least will survive to
witness the blessed change which shall
then take place on earth, when the thick
veil of ignorance shall have been removed from the eyes of our opponents,
and their minds shall have been en-
lightened to find the lost piece of silver.
May God, who overrules the destinies of

men, in His goodness and mercy bring
about this consummation!

Since I have undertaken to publish
a set treatise on the subject of Antimony,
it is fitting that I should begin with an
explanation of its name. The Arabs, to
whom this metal has long been known,
called it ASINAT; the Chaldeans designated it STIBIUM ; its usual name among
the Latins is ANTIMONY. The German
name *(Spiesglas)* reflects one of the
peculiarities of the metal, viz., the streaks
by which it is distinguished, and the ease
with which it is changed into a kind of
coloured glass.*

This variety of names teaches us
two things : first, that Antimony was
known to the Arabs, Chaldeans, Latins,

---

* Poets sometimes commence their tale in the middle, and
then work back to the beginning, in order to sustain the interest of their readers. Alchemists sometimes adopt the
same device in order that their meaning may be hidden from
all except the worthy. Here Basilius, in the middle of the
treatise, begins to discuss the name of his substance, with
which an ordinary writer would have commenced, but soon
he abandons this plan, and proceeds to answer the question,
already mooted, whether Antimony can be deprived of all
its poison,—a question which is explained by means of useful
and highly significant illustrations.

and Germans, and, second, that its virtues were held in the highest estimation
among them ; but that afterwards hereti-
cal notions crept in, the potency of
Antimony was more and more forgotten,
and its glory obscured and finally ex-
tinguished. That this should be so,
must appear very natural to any one
acquainted with the wiles and cunning
craftiness of the great Arch-enemy of our
race, who ever lies in wait to deceive the
children of men, and to rob them of the
light which they possess. And especially
does he put forth all his power in order
to induce amongst men ignorance of the
true medicine, and to discourage its use.
He knows well that thereby the glory of
God is obscured, and the sacrifice of
thanksgiving kept back which else would
rise from many a human heart to the
Giver of All, who has shed abroad among
created things the outer rays of His
glory. However, it is comparatively of
little use to speak about the name of
Antimony. Its great virtue and utility
can be known only to those who are

familiar with the method of its preparation. Hence I will rather strive to
immortalize my name by throwing as
much light as I can on this part of the
subject.

But before I attempt to declare the
virtue of Antimony, you should know
that, although Antimony in its raw state
is a deadly poison, yet poison can attract
to itself poison more effectually by far
than any other heterogeneous substance.

This assertion is proved by the fact
that the body of an unicorn, which is
entirely free from poison, repels every
poisonous thing. Place a live spider in-
side a circle formed by a strip of the skin
of an unicorn, and you will observe that
the spider will not be able to pass. But
if the circle be composed of some envenomed substance, the spider will have
no difficulty in crossing the line, which
is homogenous to its own nature.

Any similar experiment would yield
the same result. Hollow out a silver
coin, and let it float on the water like a
boat. Then hold close to it, yet without

making actual contact, a particle of a
true unicorn. The coin will be as surely
repelled and moved backward as the
duck which sees the sportsman taking
aim at it with his gun.

That homogeneous substances
always attract each other you may learn
from the fact, that if you place a piece
of pure, unadulterated bread in a bowl
of water, so that it floats on the surface,
and hold, not very far from it, a piece of
true unicorn, the bread will float in any
direction in which the piece of unicorn is
moved. So great is the attraction of
like to like in Nature that poison
always draws towards it irresistibly all
that is poisonous, and substances which
are free from venom exert the same
influence over substances which enjoy a
similar immunity.

Hence poison can be removed in
two ways : firstly, by its contrary which
repels it, as the unicorn repels the spider ; secondly, by its like, which attracts
it by magnetic power. The poison which
is to cure a homogeneous poison must

have been so prepared that it shall have become a medicine instead of a poison, in order that it may attract the other, may take it up into its own nature, and expel it.

A proof of this action of natural affinities may be observed in the effect of soap upon linen. Soap is composed of oil, fat, and other greasy substances, which seem much more likely to sully than to cleanse linen. But by means of digestion, and through the action of salt, a certain rectification and separation has taken place, so that the soap now, instead of smirching the linen, attracts to itself all the impurities with which it is defiled, and renders it clean and white. In the same way poison may be so prepared as to become instead a purifying medicine, which attracts to itself all the corruption of the human system, and restores it to perfect soundness and health.

As we have begun to point out to the true student of medicine what is good and what is evil in Nature—a question in regard to which our so-called doctors maintain a supine carelessness— it will be well to set forth the truth, and to make it plain by a few more experiments and illustrations.

Let an egg, which is congealed by the winter's frost, be placed in icy-cold water. The shell will soon be covered with ice, but the frost will be extracted from the egg, and it will be fresh and vital as before.

If any man's hand or foot be frozen, he should at once apply snow or ice-water to it. The cold will thus be extracted and the limb saved.

On the contrary, inflammation is best cured by means of some hot or burning substance. If you have an inflammation in your hand, apply to it spirit of wine (which is pure fire), or quintessence of sulphur; the outward heat will attract to itself the inward fire, and not only will you experience immediate relief, but the limb will become strong as before.

In order still further to confirm

this truth, I add yet another illustration.
Take the spawn of frogs, which is found
in March ; dry it on a plate in the sun,
place it on a wound inflicted by a viper
or other venomous serpent, and the
wound will be so prepared as to be
healed subsequently by other medicines.
Or you may spread the spawn on a linen
rag, and then apply it to the wound with
the same result.

Similarly, you may take a venomous
toad, dry it in the sun, reduce it to ashes
in a carefully closed pot, pulverize, and
apply the powder to any poisoned wound,
whereupon it will attract to itself all the
poison of the wound. Why ? By the
combustion or calcination of the toad, its
inward efficacy is called out, and becomes
operative. The principle which we have
so largely illustrated holds good in all
cases. If you are seized with the plague,
treat it with *astrum solis*, or spirit of Mercury, for the spirit of Mercury attracts
every poisonous matter, and purifies the
system of all its morbific particles.

The efficacy of *astrum solis* (Star of

the Sun) is infinitely greater. For it concentrates within itself all the quickning power of the Sun, which is the life of Nature. It is the Soul of Gold, and the generative principle of all minerals and metals. I will say more about this wonderful *astrum solis* in its own proper place.

In the same way, we must treat Antimony, which has the like operative qualities as the body of gold. I do not now speak of the Star of the Sun. " For," says Antimony, " I know that I must quake and tremble exceedingly before it, and though I greatly excel it in many principal respects, yet, on the whole, I can effect none of those things, which the Star of the Sun, strengthened by heavenly testimony, is able to accomplish. I do not speak either of the star of Mercury, whose parentage is the same as mine. But as to intense penetrative virtue, I must yield the palm to the Star of the Sun."

My books and sayings are related to each other by experience, like the metals, one of which must be tested and known in its relation to the rest. In like manner, my writings and prescriptions have one common scope or aim. The guide who alone can lead you to the place where Plutus sits enthroned, is Vulcan (the god of fire). If you strike steel with a flint, the violent collision elicits a spark, and calls forth the hidden sulphur, or hidden fire, which is kindled by the air so that it burns truly and effectually. Salt remains in the ashes, and mercury is struck out together with the burning sulphur.*

In Antimony, too, the mercury must, by a natural method, be separated from its sulphur and salt. Unless the fire which is latent in the steel becomes visible and tangible, it can be of no use ; and so our Medicine will 'produce no effect,

---

* This illustration is as remarkable and suggestive as it is simple. From cold steel there is struck out with a cold flint a tiny spark of fire, which has power to penetrate a whole mountain of fuel with intense burning flame. This phenomenon is of daily occurrence, and in it the fixed becomes volatile, and the volatile is fixed. Here is wisdom for him who has eyes to see, and an answer for those who doubt the power of Alchemy.

F

unless it be first separated from its gross elements, rectified, manifested, clarified, and prepared, that all may see how a separation of the pure from the impure has taken place, and that the pure metal is purged of all earthy elements, after which the harvest may be expected. But this cannot take place, until the metal has been opened and dissolved by a carefully regulated fire.

In order that I may comprehend much matter of importance within a small compass, this, shortly, is the sum of the science of Antimony.

Whatever is hidden from common observation is the province of Art ; but as soon as the hidden has become manifest and visible, the task of our Art is accomplished, and all that remains to be done is purely mechanical, as I have more than once set forth in my other books. '

The bee extracts honey from the flower by the art which God has given to her ; but when once the honey is visibly perfect, that sweet and fragrant

liquid can be prepared in such a way as
to become a most potent and deadly
poison. This is a fact which no one
will believe who has not seen experimental proof of it. Nevertheless, though
a corrosive poison is prepared from
honey, no one has any right to say that
honey itself is poisonous or harmful.
Here is something which may deliver
our doctors from Divine vengeance.
Honey is indirectly prepared from the
excrements of brute beasts, with which
the meadows are manured, and whence
hundred and thousands of sweet and
fragrant flowers spring up. From these
the quintessence is sucked by the bees,
whereby there takes place an alteration
and generation of one thing into another,
i.e., into an aliment of different form and
taste, resembling its former condition in
no particular, and designated honey.
This honey may be either a pleasant
form of food for man, or there may be
prepared from it a poison of the most
deadly effect, both on man and beast.

Therefore, gentle reader, whoever

and whatever you are, follow me and Nature. I will teach you the whole truth without any admixture of falsehood. I will instruct you how to distinguish truth from error, good from evil, the highest from the lowest. For though Antimony be a deadly poison, there can be prepared from it a medicine which radically destroys all diseases, and penetrates and consumes them, by coction, like fire.

First, Antimony must be prepared so as to become a true Stone, which is its quintessence. And forasmuch as in this operation it is in all things like fire, I call it, after its coagulation, the Fire Stone. When this Fire Stone has been properly prepared, according to the directions given at the end of this treatise, its medicinal virtue is such as to consume all noxious humours, purify the blood to the highest degree, and be in all things equal to the efficacy of potable gold.

Here I ask you, my inexperienced doctors, not to judge me by the standard

of your own ignorance. It is not enough
for you to read my book, and to become
acquainted theoretically with the prepar-
tion of Antimony; you must experiment-
ally follow my directions, and thus gain
the knowledge which will teach you both
how to prepare and apply this medicine.*

When you have done this, you will
begin to have some notion of that which
is now hidden from your purblind gaze.

O wretched and pitiable medicasters,
who walk on the clouds, and on mountains in the air, thinking highly of
yourselves in your own conceit, and yet
having no solid foundation for your feet,
take heed, I beseech you, what answer
you will make to God on the day of
judgment! Think of the sacred duty
which rests upon you before it is too
late, and then, if you are really willing
to do that which is right, God will most
assuredly help you. But you who, in
your extreme folly and madness, do not

---

* Here Basilius once more yields to his indignation
against the false Doctors ; but afterwards he gives some useful hints embodied in remarks on aqua fortis and spirit of
wine.

care to learn, or to become any wiser, refrain, at least, from pronouncing upon what you do not understand, lest your own judgment be harder than you can bear.

It should be the principal aim of every physician, whilst he does everything he can to cure the disease, not to hinder rather than help the cure which Nature is trying to effect. If the spirit of wine be added to aqua fortis, there will be a strong effervescence, and these two substances will not agree ; but if they be properly united, by means of philosophical distillation, they will form a highly useful compound. Oil of tartar and grape vinegar are similarly related. They are as incompatible as fire and water, although they are both prepared from the same substance. Hence it should be the physician's first care to become acquainted with all the circumstances of the disease. These circumstances he should then diligently consider, and select such remedies as are likely to remove the disorder, lest, by giving the wrong medicine, he does more harm than good. For instance, if, while iron is being dissolved in aqua fortis, you sup-denly pour into it oil of tartar, you will burst the glass vessel : for contrary quali-ties, when brought into collision, generate a consuming fire. Of these things our solemn, begowned doctors know nothing, and can conceal their ignorance only by judicious silence. To you I speak, ye solemn titular physicians, and to you, apothecaries, who fill with your concoc-tions dire pots as large as those which are used to cook soup for a hundred persons—ye that are stoneblind, pray that your eyes may be anointed with eyesalve, and that the thick scales of darkness may fall from your mind! Then you may perhaps see the truth as in a bright mirror. Pray that you may find the medicine which God has im-planted in the noblest and most precious of created things for the good of the human race, whereby we may obtain help at need, and health when laid low with sickness! Why are you, wretched worms of the dust, and food for worms, always stopping short at the husk, and neglecting the precious kernel, forgetful of your Creator, who has formed you after His own image? Why do you not rather thank Him by studying His works which transcend Nature? Return, behold in your heart the image of your ingratitude, and pray that you may feel heartily ashamed of yourself for not having realized and accepted with a thankful heart what God has prepared for you!

But I must conclude this appeal, lest, while I write, I stain the pages of my book with tears of indignation, and lest, while deploring the blindness of the world, I render these words illegible, which I wish to become known to all. I am a man belonging to a most holy religious order, in which I shall continue to live so long as God is pleased to animate this wretched body of mine with the breath of life. Hence I must needs write as becomes a religious man. But if I were a secular judge, I would lift up

my voice, and speak out in loud clarion
tones, so as to force those deaf persons to
hear who now stop their ears, and blas-
pheme, despise, and ignorantly calumni-
ate the truth.

But Thou, O Lord God, Who
dwellest on high, and art truly called the
God of Sabbaoth, Who rulest heaven and
earth, which thou hast created, Who
orderest the course of the stars, Whom
the elements obey, before Whom all creation trembles and quails, both in heaven,
on earth, and under the earth, look down,
I beseech Thee, on this world, and teach
the children of men the inner meaning of
those things which Thou hast visibly set
forth before their eyes! As for me, I
know that I am utterly unworthy of the
gifts of health and riches which Thou
hast so graciously bestowed on me. Yet,
as long as I live, I will praise and bless
Thy Holy Name. More than this, my
Father, I cannot do in this miserable and
imperfect world.

In beginning a treatise on Antimony, we must first describe the root

whence it receives all its glory and strength, and is exalted to the perfection of operation. We must shew also how it originates in the earth, after what manner it is made subject to the dominion of the stars, by which elements it is cooked, and by which led to maturity. Antimony is nothing but a vapour, or a mineral exhalation, produced by the stars above, and digested through elementary media to a state of coagulation and maturity. Observe that Antimony has originally received its virtue, essence, properties, and efficacy from the same planet as common Mercury; but its coagulation and its essence are harder. The reason is to be found in the fact that of the three principles, it has received more salt than liquid Mercury. For though salt is the least important of its three first principles, yet it has more of the essence of salt than common Mercury, and consequently a more permanent coagulation. For it is salt that imparts hardness to minerals, and an excess of hot spirit of sulphur keeps Mercury in a

liquid condition—nor can it be coagulated, unless there are added to it certain
other metallic spirits, infused by a wondrous process into the Mother of Saturn.
Without this, Mercury cannot be fixed
except by the Philosopher's Stone.
Through the mediation of the Stone,
indeed, its three principles are har-
monized, and it acquires a fusible and
malleable body. Only in this way can
the volatility of Mercury be permanently
removed.

No animal or vegetable contains
anything that can avail to fix Mercury ;
the attempt to do this has always ended
in failure, because none of these substances have a metallic nature. Mercury
is both inwardly and outwardly pure fire ;
therefore no fire can destroy it, no fire
can change its essence. It flees from the
fire, and resolves itself spiritually into
an incombustible oil ; but when it is once
fixed no cunning of man can volatilize it
again. Then everything can by art be
made of it that can be produced from gold,
because after its coagulation it perfectly

resembles gold, seeing that it has grown from the same root, and sprung from exactly the same branch as that precious metal. But just now I am not concerned with Mercury. I have proposed to myself at present to describe the true origin of Antimony. Nevertheless, what has been said of Mercury is important for the due apprehension of certain ulterior considerations, and for the clearer understanding of the nature of Antimony itself, which is sprung from the same root as Mercury.*

Let me tell you, then, that all metals and all minerals grow in the same way from the same root, and that thus all metals have a common origin. This first principle is a mere vapour extracted from the elementary earth through the heavenly planets, and, as it were, divided by the sidereal distillation of the Macrocosmos. This sidereal hot

* The great question which vexes all the students of our Art : " What is our Mercury ? " is here clearly and lucidly answered. Attend carefully to all that Basilius says. Any light that I could add to his brightness would be darkness indeed.

infusion, descending from on high into those things which are below, with the æro-sulphureous property, so acts and works as to engraft on them in a spiritual and invisible manner a certain strength and virtue. This vapour afterwards resolves itself in the earth into a kind of water, and out of this mineral water all metals are generated and perfected. The mineral vapour becomes this or that metal according as one or the other of the three first principles predominates, *i.e.*, according as they have much or little mercury, sulphur, or salt, or an unequal mixture of their weights. Hence, some metals are fixed, and some are not fixed; some are permanent and unchangeable; some are volatile and variable, as you may see in gold, silver, copper, iron, tin, and lead.

Besides these metals, other minerals are generated from these three principles; according to the proportion of the ingredients, we have vitriol, antimony, marcasite, electrum, and many other minerals.

In its very first astrum, or star, and

its first substance, gold has more perfect sulphur, and more perfect mercury than the other metals and minerals. Hence its operative virtue is much stronger and more potent, as it is also more efficacious than the stars of the other metals. The qualities which are found singly in other metals are all united, with many more, in the composition of the solar star, which is gold.

When the substance of gold is matured and perfected by fire, it embodies more perfections than all other metals and minerals together. There is only one metal (which we have already mentioned) wherein the solar sulphur is quite as potent, or even more potent than in gold. Of the two metals in which the substance strongly predominates, we can here say no more. I must remain within the limits which I have set myself, and confine my attention for the present to Antimony.

Antimony is a mineral made of a terrestrial vapour changed into water, which sidereal change is the true Star of

Antimony. This water has been extracted from elementary earth by the stars
and the fire which is contained in the
air. Through coagulation it has then
become a tangible essence. This tangible essence encloses a large quantity
of predominating sulphur ; after it comes
mercury, and of salt there is least of all,
yet it has enough salt to make it hard
and immalleable.

Its chief quality is hot and dry—of
frigidity and humidity it has very little
indeed. The same is true of common
Mercury, and of gold, which has more
heat than frigidity.

Enough has been said about the
substance and the three radical principles
of Antimony, as also of its perfection
by the Archæus in elementary earth.
Students of Alchemy do not care to be
told where to find the Star to whose
influence Antimony is subjected ; they
rather desire to be instructed in its preparation and its uses. They wish to be
able to test for themselves the truth of
all the wonders that have been related of

Antimony at all times by men of all classes. Both the learned and the un-learned look directly for satisfaction of this their burning and insatiable desire. Therefore, I will not try the patience of my readers by any unnecessary delay, but will briefly set forth the results of my diligent researches as to the nature of Antimony, though human life is too short for any one to be fully acquainted with all its secrets. For in the pre-paration of Antimony miracle follows on miracle, colour upon colour, and the potency and operation of each succeeding degree is greater than that which went before.

To begin with, Antimony is a rank and deadly poison, which may cause the death of men and beasts, so thoroughly has the destructive essence pervaded every part of this mineral. Hence the universal outcry, which is raised both by the vulgar and by those doctors who are ignorant of the real nature of Medi-cine. All exclaim with one accord : "Poison, poison, poison!" Now we do

not advise any one to apply common
Antimony as a Medicine, because its use
would really be fatal to health and life.
Both at the courts of the princes and in
towns the brethren of the profession
warn kings, courtiers, and burghers not
to have anything to do with Antimony.
This outcry has actually brought the
substance into evil repute, and to this
very day no one ventures to avail himself of the wonderful and various medicinal qualities latent therein. Yet I
solemnly declare, in the presence of God,
the Creator of heaven and earth, and of
things both visible and invisible, which
we either know now or shall one day
know, that there is not beneath the
sun any more efficacious Medicine, or
stronger pillar of health, than this very
same Antimony.

Hearken diligently to my words,
and ye, wise men of this world, observe
well the announcement which I shall
make concerning Antimony : for my
theory is based upon Nature, and my
practice on experience. I am fully pre-

G

pared to admit, and I have already admitted, that, before its preparation, Antimony is a poison, and nothing else. Nevertheless, you Doctor, or Master of Arts, or Bachelor of Arts, or whatever your title, on the strength of which you speak ignorantly and arrogantly about things which you do not understand : listen carefully to my words, and hearken to what I have to say to you.

Antimony, you affirm, is a poison : therefore let every one beware of using it ! But this conclusion is not logical, Sir Doctor, Magister, or Baccalaureus ; it is not logical, Sir Doctor, however much you may plume yourself on your red cap. Theriac is prepared from the venom of the viper, the most deadly poison in the world. Does it therefore follow that Theriac ought not to be used as a Medicine? You know that it is so employed ; and, similarly, Antimony can be so freed of its poison by our Spagyric Art as to become a most salutary Medicine, just as the viper's poison acquires medicinal properties after its conversion into Theriac. Without preparation, indeed, Antimony can do no good, but only harm.

Whoever desires to become a disciple of Antimony, let him, after earnest prayer and calling upon God, betake himself to the school of Vulcan (fire), who is the Master and Revealer of all arcana. This teacher is scorned and despised by the wise of this world, because, through their own carelessness and stupidity, they have learned nothing of him. Yet no medicine can possibly be prepared without Vulcan, whatever any persons, in their ignorance and senseless arrogance, may affirm to the contrary.

But I must now proceed to declare the processes by which Antimony is prepared. I know that I shall meet with loud and sustained opposition. But I do not care ; I will ask my opponents one question, and one only : Can they produce anything that is better than Antimony, seeing that from Antimony it is possible to prepare medicines equal to those

which exist in gold and mercury, with
the exception of the Star of Sol? From
this can be prepared potable gold
(against leprosy), spirit of mercury (that
sovereign remedy for the French disease),
and many other medicines. I pity the
ignorance of our adversaries, for they
speak of those things which they do not
understand, and, therefore, no weight
whatever can attach to their words. In
vain would the stable boy attempt to
teach the donkey to tune his voice to
sweet harmonious music, for he cannot
learn. In our Art only those are
qualified to deliver a sound opinion who
have listened to the voice of experience.
Any other person, whatever high-sound-
ing title may be attached to his name,
is no better than an ignoramus and a
charlatan.

But, before I go on to the practical
part of this treatise, someone may ask :
How minerals and metals come to contain
poison? What poison is? How anything
can be purified, and have its envenomed
nature removed? These and similar

enquiries I desire first to answer briefly and clearly.

The origin of poison is either natural or supernatural. One reason why God has implanted poison in created things was His purpose to shew us His wonders, and to teach us how to distinguish good from evil— how to choose the good and eschew the evil.

In the same way the tree of life was set in Paradise. Its proper use would have tended to our benefit. Its abuse brought about our fall, and all the suffering that has followed from it.

The second reason that there is such a thing as poison is God's purpose that we should thereby learn the ugliness and hatefulness of evil, and conceive a desire to substitute that which is good in its place. For God hates nothing that He has made, but rather desires our moral and physical amendment. By eschewing poison we are to be taught how to avoid the evil and choose the good.

Poison is also produced by contrary oppositions and conjunctions among the stars, which infect the elements, and are the cause of the plague and other contagious diseases in this nether world. This is clearly seen in the case of comets.

Poison is further occasioned by hostile extremes—for instance, by excessive anger, or by drinking cold water when you are very hot. Deadly weapons may also be enumerated among causes of poison, though when used in self-defence, they are rather of the nature of medicines.

The natural origin of poison is as follows. Whatever is repugnant to Nature is poison; as, for instance, if anyone takes food which does not agree with him, that food is poison, because repugnant to his nature. Yet to another with whom it may agree, it is medicine.

But poison is specially attracted to bodies in the earth, where a certain crude, undigested mercurial essence (I speak of mineral poisons), which has not yet undergone any proper coction, so

pervades the whole body as to make it a
crude, immature, undigested mineral.
For instance, if a man were to eat raw
grain, his stomach would be too feeble
to digest it, because it has not sufficient
natural heat. Grain which is first digested
by the fire of the great world, must be still
further digested by the little fire, in order
to be easy of digestion in our little world.
It is the same with raw meat—and,
similarly, crude Antimony is not yet
sufficiently digested to be capable of
assimilation by a feeble human stomach.
All cathartics, both animal and vegetable, as well as mineral, contain a certain
volatile, undigested Mercury. This volatility is the cause that all other things
in the human stomach are expelled by a
cathartic, though the root of the disease
itself is left untouched, and can be removed only by a fixed medicine. Only
fixed medicines can cope with fixed
diseases, but these purgatives are like
water dashed on the pavement, which
cleans the stones outwardly, though it
does not enter them. Fixed medicines

attack the seat of the disease, and are
not content with a mere external wash-
ing away of impurities. Hence we
admonish all and sundry that Antimony
has to be freed of its crudeness and
poisonous indigestibility before it can be
safely applied as a medicine ; and this
transformation is effected by fire, and by
fire only. Vulcan is the only arbiter of
such a purifying process. What Vulcan
(fire) of the upper sphere has left crude
and unfinished is accomplished by the
Vulcan of the lower world. He matures
the immature, digests the crude with his
heat, and separates the pure from the
impure. By the separation and fire
which perfect fixation, its poisonous
nature is removed, and all that is evil in
Antimony is changed into something
good. Fire purges away the deadly
nature of our medicine, as is known only
to those who have fraternally co-opera-
ted with Vulcan, and have seen the bride
cleansed of all impurity in the fiery bath,
which enables her to lie in the bridal bed
with her chosen spouse.

Woe unto you, who neither understand, nor care to understand my words! If you knew the meaning of fixation and volatility, and of the separation of pure and impure, you would cease from your foolish occupation and follow me alone. It is I, Antimony, that speak to you. In me you find mercury, sulphur, and salt, the three great principles of health. Mercury is in the regulus, sulphur in the red colour, and salt in the black earth which remains. Whoever can separate these, and then re-unite and fix them by art, without the poison, may truly call himself blessed; for he has the Stone, which is called fire, and in the Stone, which can be composed out of Antimony, he has the means of perfect health and temporal subsistence.

In Antimony you will find all colours, black, white, red, green, blue, and an incredible number of mixed tints (besides grey and yellow), which must all be severally known, and used in their own proper order.

Now I will declare how the medicine should be prepared and fixed, and how all that is good in it may be increased, and all that is bad diminished and destroyed.

Here let me advertise the lover of art that the virtue of Antimony is not one among many precious stones, but it combines the virtues of all other precious stones, as is sufficiently evidenced by its colours. Its red represents carbuncle, pyropus, and coral ; its white, diamond and crystal ; its blue, sapphire ; its green, emerald ; its yellow, jacynth ; its black, granite. As to the metals, its black corresponds to Saturn, its red to iron, its yellow to gold, its green to copper, its blue to silver, its white to mercury, its mixed colours to tin. And not only does Antimony contain the colours, it also contains the virtues and qualities of all other stones and metals, only human life is too short for any one to learn how to educe all the potencies that lie concealed in the heart of Antimony. You may get from it, by distillation, an acid humour, like pure vinegar. By another way, you may prepare a red pellucid substance, as sweet as refined sugar or honey—or you may obtain a bitter substance, like absynth—or an acid substance, like salt oil. At one time it is red, yellow, or white, and is borne upward like a flying eagle. Then, again, it exhibits various colours, and is driven downwards, and, by reverberation, becomes a metal, like lead. Sometimes it looks like transparent glass of a red, yellow, black, white, or variegated colour. All of these it is inadvisable to use in medicines unless they have been subjected to some other test. It may also become a variety of subtle oils, whose medicinal virtue transcends their outward appearance ; their use is chiefly for applications to wounds and ulcers. The manifold variations which it undergoes might puzzle the oracle of Delphi.

Out of it we may evolve living mercury, and sulphur which burns like common sulphur ; moreover, a grey powder can be prepared from it, with real natural salt and many other things.

We will therefore now speak of its preparations, its magistery, arcanum, and tincture, its elixir, and its special essence, which you will be able to extract when I have told you about the Fire-Stone and its preparation, and many other arcana and secrets, of which the wise men of this world know nothing, and to which too little attention has been paid since the decay of the Egyptians, Arabs, and Chaldeans. These truths are of the greatest importance in the study of the true medicine.

Take care that the different operations shall follow each other in the exact order in which I declare and describe ; for if the result is to be perfection, every part of the work must be properly attended to. Now, fixed medicines expel and eradicate fixed diseases ; but Antimony, in its crude state, is only a purgative, which does not touch the real root of the disease.

I will therefore declare the preparation of all things which belong to Antimony ; I will deliver up the keys thereof, and earnestly ask the student to bear in mind that fire is the sure key by which access is obtained to most of the secrets of our Art. This mineral preparation of Antimony is prepared in various manners by the regimen of fire and by a multiple manual operation, whence its medicinal activity, virtue, potency, and colour flow and emanate.

As Antimony is distinguished by a crude, black colour, variegated with white, I will now speak of the first operation to which the substance is subjected, viz., calcination, or incineration, which is carried out in the following manner :

Take best Hungarian Antimony, or any kind you can get ; pulverize it as finely as possible, spread thinly on an earthenware dish (round or square) provided with a low margin ; place the dish on a calcinatory furnace over a coal fire, which should at first be moderate. As soon as you see smoke rise from the Antimony, stir it about with an iron spoon, and continue doing so till there is no more smoke, and the Antimony sticks together in the shape of small globules. Remove it from the fire, pulverize again into a fine powder, place it on fire, and calcine, as before, till there is no more smoke. This calcination must be repeated not only till the Antimony gives out no more smoke, but does not conglomerate into globules, and has the appearance of ' pure white ashes. Then has the calcination of Antimony been successfully completed.

Place this calcined Antimony in a crucible, such as goldsmiths use for melting gold and silver, and set it over a violent fire, either lighted in a wind furnace or increased by means of the bellows, till the Antimony becomes liquid like pure water. To test whether Antimony has acquired its proper glassy transparency, dip in it an oblong piece of cold iron, and examine the Antimony which clings to it carefully. If it be clear, pure, and transparent, it is all right, and has attained its due maturity. The tyro, or beginner, should know (these remarks are addressed to beginners who are students of the Spagyric

Art) that glass, whether prepared from metals, minerals, or any other substance, must be subjected to heat, till it has attained to maturity, and exhibits a clear and pellucid transparency. Let all and several remember that that maturity and this transparency are performed solely by Vulcan operating on the secret and concealed nature. Otherwise, it is unprofitable for any further medicinal development.*

When Antimony has become vitrified in the way described, heat a flat,

abstracha Receipt 4

---

* It is obvious that Basilius is here writing for beginners— so clearly and circumstantially does he describe the very rudiments of the work. Yet even veterans may now and then find it no easy task to put his directions into practice. In such difficulties I hope that my commentary may prove useful. I have paid for the experience which it contains with much time, labour, and expense ; and therefore I have thought it my duty to warn and instruct those who after me should travel the same road. I cannot say that I greatly pity people whose minds are set only on wealth ; but I do wish to help those who have undertaken this study for the sake of their suffering neighbours. Such persons I exhort to read my commentary : for one word from me may often save them endless trouble and expense. Such a warning in time might frequently have been worth several thousand florins to me. I do not undertake to give elementary instructions to the beginner, but only to remove certain obstacles out of the way of the student.

broad copper dish over the fire, pour into it the Antimony in as clear and thin a state as possible, and you will have pure, yellow, pellucid glass of Antimony. This preparation of what I call the glass of Antimony is the simplest, best, and most efficacious with which I am acquainted.*

---

* This is a now familiar way of preparing glass of Antimony. It is serviceable in many cases of illness, but (so precarious a thing is the human constitution) its use may now and then, in one case out of a hundred, be attended with fatal results. I once saw a man who had taken a quantity give up the ghost after much vomiting and violent purging. Such casualties give a handle to the enemies of Alchemy, but the medicine in question is administered only by unscrupulous pseudo-Alchemists, who do not mind how many people they kill, so long as they cure some, and gain for themselves the reputation of great doctors. The fact is, that the emetic virtue of Antimony inheres in its salt, which salt harbours all its poisonous qualities. Hence feeble persons derive more harm from its poison than good from its medicinal properties. But if Antimony produces beneficial results even when it still has an admixture of poison, how much more beneficial is it when the poison has been removed. The following is a recipe for the glass of Antimony, which may be used without any fear of fatal results:

Take the pure glass of Antimony (of Basilius), melt in crucible till one-third part evaporates, pound into fine powder, pour on it best rectified spirit of wine, which must cover the powder to the height of three inches, close, allow to circulate for three months, and extract spirit of wine by distillation. If the tincture be red, as it will be invariably should the operation have been rightly conducted, decant it

Glass of Antimony may also be prepared with an admixture of borax, as follows :

Take one part of crude Antimony and two of Venetian borax ; pound finely, place in crucible, melt them together in a reverberatory furnace, or by a fire kept up with the bellows, pour into hot copper dish, and prepare as before ; you will then have a beautiful, pellucid Antimony like pyropus.*

The redness of this Antimony may be extracted by means of spirit of wine.†

---

and set it apart as an excellent medicine. Once more place the body which remains in a crucible, and melt and mould into whatever manner you please. In artistic shapes it may be worn as an ornament on a ring. This substance, when dissolved overnight in a glass of wine, will act as a gentle purgative or emetic if taken by a sick person the next morning. The dose (two ounces or less) must be adapted to the strength of the patient.

* This colour is only obtained by a very powerful fire.

† Not common spirit of wine, which would be useless for this operation, but that of the Sages, which is prepared as follows for the extraction of this tincture : Take four ounces of thrice-sublimed salt of ammonia ; of spirit of wine distilled over salt of tartar, so that it is quite clear—ten ounces ; place in phial over digestive fire till the spirit of wine is filled with the fire or sulphur of the salt of ammonia, distil thrice in the

H

Transparent white glass of Antimony, after its commixture, is further prepared as follows: Pound, together, one part of Antimony till it becomes a fine powder, and four parts of Venetian borax ; melt in crucible till the substances are in flux, when they will become first yellow, and then white as glass, for, under the continuous regimen of the fire, the yellow here gives place to the white, and a beautiful glass results. The white colour is matured as before, and is tested, in like manner, by the insertion of a piece of cold iron.

There are many other ways in which Antimony may be vitrified.* I only describe the results of my own practical experience, and the first way of preparing Antimony, or glass of Antimony, is

---

alembic, and you have our true menstruum, whereby the red colour is extracted out of glass of Antimony. The tincture of this glass is also extracted by means of its own vinegar, and thence, in this last operation, is obtained a most excellent medicine.

* The curious reader may find such methods in Hartmann, Crollius, Beguinus, and others.

the very best that can be conceived for all practical purposes. We thus purge out the black colour, which has evaporated in a volatile form through the chimney. Nevertheless, the Antimony still retains a considerable amount of its poisonous nature, and I will now proceed to declare to you how the poison is separated from the medicine, the pure from the impure, in return for which instruction I expect the everlasting gratitude of all my readers, and the approbation of all discerning men in every part of the world.

The first separation of sulphur from its body, and the extraction of the Tincture from its salt, are performed as follows :

Take pure glass of Antimony prepared in the first way, and uncombined with any foreign matter ; pound it as fine as the finest flour, and place in a broad-bottomed glass vessel, called Cucurbit.*

---

* In order that the powder may be as fine as required, mix the Antimony with some distilled vinegar into a thickish paste, and pound in a mortar of porphyry.

Pour over the Antimony some highly rectified vinegar, subject to digestive fire, or, in summer, expose to the rays of the sun, shaking it once and again every day.*

Let this slow digestion be continued till the vinegar assumes a yellow, or rather a reddish, colour, like that of well purified gold. Then pour off this clear and pure extracted substance, add more vinegar, and repeat the same process till no more gold-coloured Tincture can be extracted. Mix all the extract, filter, place in cucurbit, put on lid, distil the vinegar in S. Mary's Bath, till there remains at the bottom a gold-coloured powder approaching red ; pour on this powder distilled rain water ; let it evaporate by distillation, add more rain water,

---

* When I followed this latter direction literally, the substance became solid like a stone, and stuck to the bottom of the vessel, so that I could not get it off. At length, being warned by experience, I shook the vessel five or six times daily, stirring the substance with a wooden spoon, and you will be wise if you profit by my experience in this matter, not only as regards the present experiments, but in the preparation of the glass, and in every extraction of the tincture of Antimony.

and repeat this till all the acidity is washed out, and there remains a sweet and pleasant powder.*

This sweet powder you should pound in a hot marble or glass mortar, place in cucurbit, pour on it best highly rectified spirit of wine till it covers the powder to the height of three inches ; expose to gently digestive heat, as above, and there will be extracted a beautiful red Tincture with an earthy sediment at the bottom.

---

* The Author's directions are correct, but if you have much extract, you must take a large vessel ; yet the vessel should not be larger than the quantity of the extract requires —else the fire necessary to bring about the distillation will h.ve to be fiercer than the Tincture can bear. When two-thirds of the Tincture have evaporated, change the vessel, and distil the remaining Tincture in a smaller vessel, till there is left a thickish paste. If you drain the powder altogether of moisture, it will be burned. The method by which you may know whether the powder is as sweet and free from acid taste as it should be, is to taste a little of the water which you have drained off by evaporation. If you are not careful, however, you may still make a mistake, and spoil everything. For you must distinguish carefully between the acidity of the vinegar and the acidity of the Antimony ; else you may go on with the distillation after all the acidity of the vinegar has been removed, and distil all the acidity, *i.e.*, all the strength out of the Antimony.

The extract is sweet and pleasant to the taste ; the sediment still retains its poisonous character, but the Tincture is a wonderfully potent external Remedy, both for man and beast, passing almost the possibility of belief in any one who is inexperienced in this matter.

Three or four grains of this medicine will cure leprosy, and the new French disease. It purifies the blood, dispels melancholy, resists every poison, removes asthma and all chest complaints, including difficulty of breathing, and relieves the stitch in the side. Moreover, this Remedy cures many other diseases, if it be properly applied.*

The yellow powder mentioned above, from which the extract has not yet been

---

* This Medicine, which has no violent cathartic or purgative effects, acts gently on our spirits, imparting to them the Universal Spirit of Nature, and insensibly restoring the whole organism to perfect health. But before its purification it is like a jewel on a dung heap, and utterly unable to manifest or exhibit its virtue. The Tincture spoken of in the text has all the virtue ascribed to it by the Author. But its use should be continued for some time, in order to secure its full benefits.

made by means of spirit of wine, should
be pounded on a hot stone, and placed in
an egg, boiled hard, from which the yolk
has been taken out ; leave the powder in
a humid place, till it is dissolved into a
yellow liquid. This Tincture, used as a
liniment, is an excellent remedy for all
fresh wounds and bruises. The wound
should be painted with it by means of a
soft feather, and then bandaged with
clean linen. The cure will be effected
without putrefaction, inflammation, or
suppuration, and that so completely as
to call forth adoration and thanks unto
Him who hath created heaven and earth,
and hath permitted such a medicine to
exist therein.*

You may use this extract or balm of
Antimony for the cure of all inveterate,
inflamed, or corrosive wounds, and it will
never fail you ; lupus and cancer yield to
it ; so does caries, and the most malignant

---

* Take care, in removing the yolk, not to tear or disturb
the thin pellicle which separates the white from the yolk—or
else your Tincture will get mixed with albumen and the
greater part will be lost to you.

and neglected of ulcers, even those that
are alive with worms cannot withstand
it.*

I am acquainted with two methods
of reducing the glass of Antimony to an
oil by means of distillation in the alembic.
Take glass of Antimony, just as it is,
composed from the minera of Antimony,
pound to fine powder, extract its tincture
by means of distilled vinegar, remove all
traces of acidity (as above), add spirit of
wine, and circulate in a pelican vessel,
well closed, for a month ; dexterously

---

* If our Surgeons believed the words of Basilius, how
eager they would be to obtain this balm of Antimony ! And,
indeed, the Author rather underrates the virtues of this
remedy than otherwise, as I myself can testify. A woman
of 40 years had for seven years suffered from a hard
malignant swelling in her left breast. All the Doctors and
Surgeons whom she consulted declared her disease to be an
aggravated case of cancer. A most celebrated physician
said that the only means of cure was the amputation of the
breast. To this doubtful and desperate course the woman
would not consent, and, as a last resource, she came to me.
I thought that, in an extreme instance like this, where one
breast was twice as large as the other, and filled with
cancerous matter, I might venture to employ the balm of
Antimony, even for a disease in which Basilius does not
authorize its use. The upshot of the matter was that, in less
than two months, the woman was restored to perfect health.

distil it,* without adding anything, and you will have a red oil, from which the Fire Stone is afterwards formed, which, also, is a sweet, pleasant, and wonderful Medicine.

Receipt 10

This oil is the quintessence, or the highest form of Antimony. There must be four preparations before Antimony is perfect, and the fifth point of consideration is its USES and its APPLICATION to the human body. The first preparation is calcination and liquefaction into glass;

abstract

---

* The great difficulty which puzzled me for many years, is how to bring about this dexterous distillation. Shall I describe it to you in a riddle ? Haste slowly ; "a bitch in a hurry brings forth blind pups." By mean of Bacchus, Juno, and Vulcan, you must give your substance wings, but restrain it from flying away. Let Mercury instruct it in the Art of flying. Hold it at first by a string, lest it rise upward beyond your reach before the time and fall headlong, like Icarus, with scorched wings. In due season, you may suffer it to spread its wings, for then it will wing its flight to the Isles of the Blest. Do you accuse me of mocking you after the manner of Tantalus? What would you have ? I may not cast pearls before swine, or lightly make the mystery of mysteries the common property of fools and knaves. Those who understand the Art, understand me. If you do not understand me, ponder, read, and study the books of the Sages ; compare their parables with mine, and you will see that I have shed much additional light on the subject.

the second is digestion, by which the extract is perfected ; the third is coagulation ; the fourth is its distillation into an oil, the subtle being separated from the gross. Then follows fixation by the last coagulation, and thereby you obtain the pellucid fiery Stone – which can operate on metals only when it is fermented, and rendered penetrative. Even so, it can only act in a particular manner, as I shall explain further on, when I speak of the Fire Stone.

The distilled oil, of which I have spoken, accomplishes all purposes for which it can be employed by the phy sician.*

---

* If I did not know that Basilius is here declaring no more than the bare truth, I should take him for one of the quacks and mountebank charlatans of the market place. But experience has taught me that he rather understates than exaggerates his case. If you do not believe me, the way is open for you to try. I repeat that this Oil, if properly used, is truly an Universal Medicine. The body must, however, first have been purged of its gross humours by means of general remedies. Moreover, there are some diseases which are incurable, and I do not say that our Oil is of any avail against these. I have the most irrefragable evidence that this medicine acts like magic in all fever, and especially the quartan fever, the reproach of the old system. In 1665 I cured a

The proper dose of this oil before coagulation is eight grains dissolved in pure wine. It restores youth and dispels melancholy ; the hair and the nails are renewed, and the whole frame is renovated, as the Phœnix is said to be renovated by fire. It destroys all adverse symptoms like a consuming fire, but itself cannot be consumed by fire ; its action is as universal as that of potable gold. The Star of the Sun, if properly fixed, alone excels all other remedies ; for the Star of the Sun and the Star of Mercury arise from one

---

very bad case of dropsy (a girl of twenty-one) by two doses of this medicine daily for twenty days ; at the end of that period the body had been reduced to its proper dimensions by means of profuse perspirations and other modes of excretion. Notice, O lover of learning, should you chance to prepare it yourself, or to receive it prepared by another, that this oil does not imitate the operation of other diaphoretics, the first dose of which provokes perspiration. But if it be placed in a body obstructed by humours, the first dose effects nothing, except slowly opening the pores ; on the second day it gently stimulates perspiration ; on the third day there is profuse sweating ; on the fourth day water is removed from the system in large quantities. But this is a matter for the physicians ; the Key of Hercules is useless if it be not in the hands of Hercules.

mother's blood, and from one fountain of vitalizing health.*

No one need be afraid that this oil of Antimony, distilled with vinegar, afterwards with the purest spirit of wine, then most skilfully extracted, and, lastly, though of all most important, exalted by means of fire, will ever act as a purgative ; it purifies the body by means of perspiration, and by means of urinary and salivary excretions.

Common glass of Antimony is pulverized ; six grains or more are absolved in warm wine overnight ; in the morning the wine is drunk without the sediment, and purges, both by laxation and vomiting, on account of the poisonous crudeness which still remains in glass of Antimony.† It is impossible

---

* The gold and the Mercury here spoken of are not the common metals, but the gold and Mercury of the Sages, more precious by far than is any ordinary metal, more powerful than all other Mercury, that even which was fabled to restore the dead to life. Therefore, I advise you not rashly to spend your money on that which cannot profit.

† This emetic is now commonly used by all quacks, but not always with happy results. It is as with the sword of brave Scanderbeg, the Castriot. The Sultan Mahomet

that I should be acquainted with all the secrets of Antimony, as my life is short, and I am only a man ; but even in the grave I will praise you, if by careful study and experiment you succeed in improving upon and supplementing my discoveries. Common glass of Antimony may be reduced into an oil, which will be quite safe, and of great value, in epileptic cases, as I shall at once proceed to explain.

Pound the glass of Antimony into as fine a powder as possible, add omphacium, digest for some days in a broad-bottomed cucurbit well-closed with clay,

Receipt 12

---

desired to see this miraculous sword which had wrought such wonders in the battlefield. But when it was sent to him, he could perceive nothing remarkable about it. "No wonder," said a courtier, "for Scanderbeg has sent his sword, but he has not sent his arm." The best medicine in unskilled hands may produce fatal results. In order to be quite safe, I prepare this emetic as follows : ℞. Four ounces of pure glass of Antimony, and half-an-ounce of Venetian borax ; melt them together, when you will have a green glossy substance like emerald ; pound fine, and put into French wine ; keep it in a warm place for some days ; then give to the patient, according to his strength, one to two ounces of this mixture. This emetic is quite safe, and if you pour more wine on the sediment it will be just as efficacious an emetic as the first.

A note to receipt 11

till all the moisture is abstracted ; pound with a double quantity of clarified sugar, moistened with spirit of vinegar ; place in a retort, and distil, in the name of God, at the end, with a strong fire ; you will then have a red oil—which must be clarified to transparency with spirit of wine.*

To this oil add a little spirit of salt, and pour the whole into a subtle preparation of "calx of gold," which has previously been prepared with its water, after a manner which I have laid down in my other writings ; it will then transcend the alembic. When they are thus distilled together, it assumes the Tincture of gold, and leaves the body intact.†

---

* This process is somewhat difficult. Basilius would say that the oil must be carried across the alembic. It is the "dexterous distillation" which I explained to you above.

† Do you understand the riddle, my friend? You cannot understand it, unless there come an Œdipus to solve it for you, or an Alexander to cut the Gordian Knot. The difficulty lies in the fact that all solvents by which tinctures are extracted must themselves be colourless ; for, unless they are so, how can you know whether you have really extracted the Tincture, or only recovered your solvent? I will tell you briefly how I carried out this operation in the year 1665. I rectified the red oil in the retort, and obtained a white oil of

When this fermentation has taken place, the medicine which results is so wonderfully efficacious that I might fill several books with an enumeration of its virtues.

But any physician, who will dili-

---

a pleasant acid taste ; I poured to it half as much spirit of salt, digested the two together for a month in a retort, in order to effect their conjunction, and then still further amal-gamated them by distillation ; then I poured them on the calx of gold, and digested the mixture for a month, till it was of a golden colour, approaching red. Thereupon, I gently poured out the tincture, and softly removed the moisture after it had been placed in a retort. A reddish powder then re-mained at the bottom, which I sweetened with distilled rain water, and again extracted the Tincture with spirit of wine. Then I restored that winged red dragon, gave him his tail to eat for six whole months, and obtained a most sweet and pleasant Tincture, ten or twelve grains of which remove, by means of perspiration, the morbific matter of every curable disease. The solvent which is employed must not only be sweet and free from corrosive properties, it must also be of a nature homogeneous with that of the substance on which it is poured, in order that it may extract from the mercury of the body a good and pure sulphur. Rectified spirit of wine is the most congenial to the sulphur of our substance, which does not amalgamate with the spirit of salt. But as to the Tincture which is obtained in this way, you must not suppose for a moment that it is the Potable Gold of the Sages. That would be a serious mistake. The Tincture is most precious, but it has only the colour, and not the weight of potable gold. About this potable Tincture of Gold it is not my business to speak in this place.

gently, and philosophically consider the subject, will discover fresh virtues in this Medicine every day, and will learn more from its use than from his whole Pharmacopœia beside.

When you have prepared Antimony to this point, you may justly boast that you have solved the enigma of the Sages, and that you have learned the Magistery which is known only to few.

This Magisterium, when mixed with a solution or tincture of corals, and taken in some cordial water, heals all diseases which proceed from some impure condition of the blood, strengthens the nerves, promotes chastity and goodness, and makes a man fit for every business which he takes in hand.

We should, therefore, at all times thank the Creator for implanting such wonderful virtues in created things, and for supplying us with the means of dispelling every disease and weakness.

We will now briefly continue our instruction concerning the Arcana of Antimony.

Take one part, of finely pulverized
Antimony, and *one part of* pulverized salt-armo-
niac,* so called because it comes from
Armenia; mix these together, place
in a retort, and distil together.† On
the product of this distillation pour hot,
distilled (common) rain water, removing
thereby every salt and acrid taste. Then
the Antimony will be of a pure, brilliant,
and feathery white; dry with subtle heat,
place in the circulatory vessel called
pelican, pour to it highly rectified spirit
of vitriol, and circulate till they are
properly amalgamated.‡ Then distil

Receipt 13 (handwritten)

---

* The quantities of the two should be equal.

† The retort should be of the kind exhibited on page
114, consisting of A Furnace, B Retort, C Receiver, D Tube,
between Receiver and Alembic E. F is a furnace which
sublimes by its moderate heat all that is in the Receiver into
Alembic E ; and so the substance which is distilled from the
Retort B is immediately sublimed by the fire of the furnace
F. This retort is useful in every kind of sublimation.

‡ This union must be so close that in distillation the
two shall rise together, otherwise you will lose both your
oil and your labour. Amalgamation in Alchemy is not
merely mixing two liquids : the union must be inseparable,
and the ingredients must really change and modify each
other. The union should be like that of male and female
seed, which produces a real organism, that is, something more
than a mere mixture of the two ingredients. Later on in

Note A to (handwritten)
Receipt (handwritten)

I

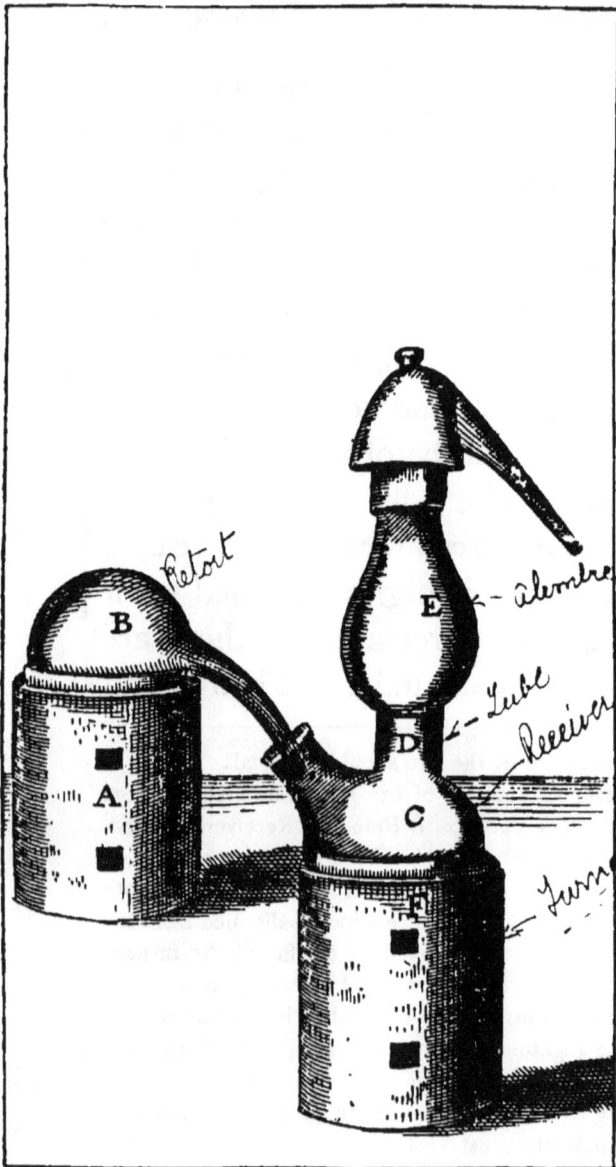

Retort

B

A

alembic

E

Tube

D

Receiver

C

F

Furnace

together, pour to mixture spirit of wine, and circulate again. Remove the sediment, which will have settled at the bottom, and you will then have the arcanum thoroughly amalgamated with the spirits of vitriol and of wine. When this arcanum has been rectified a final time, one drop of it mixed with rose water has greater medicinal value than a whole potful of herbs; it is a good appetizer and digestive, purifies the blood, and cures colic as by magic.

After the arcanum of Antimony comes its Elixir.* In the name of the Lord, take some good minera of Antimony, pulverize it finely, sublime with half as much salt of ammonia; put all that is sublimed into a glass retort, distil thrice (always removing sediment), abstract salt by edulcoration, reverberate

---

this work I give a drawing of the vessel in which I effect this union between different substances. Spirit of wine easily unites with other substances, but is as easily separated from them.

* This operation is easy, and we say nothing about it, to shew that we have not written our commentary for the purpose of putting ourselves forward.

the Antimony over a moderate fire in a well-closed vessel, till it becomes red, add strong distilled vinegar of wine, extract its redness, remove vinegar, till there remains a powder (by means of S. Mary's Bath). Extract with spirit of wine, so as to remove the sediment : you will then have a clear and pure Tincture. Place this spirit of wine with the tincture in a broad-bottomed cucurbit, add some tincture of corals, and quintessence of rhubarb, and administer a dose of three or four drops. It acts as a painless purgative, and has an exhilarating effect on the animal spirits.

Some physician may wonder that a mixture of Antimony and rhubarb, which are both violent in their action, should answer for a gentle laxative. Let such an one know that purified Antimony does not affect the bowels at all ; the purgative action proceeds from the rhubarb, which is rendered more soothing by the Antimony. By means of the clearance which the rhubarb effects, the Antimony is enabled to work more successfully on the system.*

The Elixir prepared in this way has the same power of penetrating and pervading the body with its purifying properties, that Antimony has of penetrating and purifying gold. If I were to count up and describe all its virtues, I should have to ask God to grant me a longer life, in order that I might be able to explore so many wonderful properties.

In fulfilment of my promise, I here describe those experiments which I have myself carried out. It would not become me to speak of that which I do not know. I have quite enough to do to commemorate that of which I have had practical experience. There is plenty of scope for those who come after me to investigate the marvels of Antimony. No one is more acutely sensible than myself

---

* The difference between the purgatives of Medicine and the purgatives of Alchemy is as follows : the former cause violent purging, but have no power to set up a curative process; the latter possess the double virtue both of purging and healing.

that I have by no means exhausted the subject.

This much, however, I have proved beyond a possibility of doubt – that Antimony not only purifies gold, and frees it from all foreign matter, while it also ameliorates all other metals, but it does the same for animal bodies, as regards both men and brutes. I may illustrate this by a simple experiment. If a man wishes to fatten a pig, let him give to the pig, two or three days before he begins to fatten it, half a drachm of crude Antimony, so as to cause a thorough cleaning out of the bowels ; the pig will then eat more freely, fatten more quickly, and be freed from any bilious or leprous disease to which he may be subject.

This illustration may seem somewhat unpolished and unsavoury to the great ; but it has the strong recommendation of being familiar and apposite, and of rendering the matter really clear to the general body of my readers. Of course, I do not advocate that crude Antimony should be administered to human beings : the brutes can digest raw flesh, and many other things which would overpower the strength of the human stomach. Amongst different individuals of the human family, there are also constitutional and other differences, which tax the skill and knowledge of the physician in determining the quantity that will be relatively suitable for a strong young man and a feeble old woman.

I will now proceed to speak of the further preparation and fixation of Antimony. Antimony, in its fixed state, resembles the spirit of wine which is separated from its body, and warms the body of man inwardly, while, if applied outwardly, it attracts to itself all the heat of an inflamed part. But wine which has become vinegar cools both inwardly and outwardly. Yet both spirit of wine and vinegar are preparations of the same substance.

The reason of this difference is that vinegar has undergone only digestion, *i.e.*, putrefaction of the wine, with vegetable fixation. But the spirit of wine is prepared by separation, *i.e.*, distillation, or vegetable sublimation, which renders the spirit volatile. In the same way, Antimony has different effects in accordance with the difference of its preparation.

Its fixation is brought about in the following manner : Pulverize some Antimony, place it in a broad-bottomed distilling-vessel, namely, in a cucurbit, pour upon it aqua fortis to the height of six inches, close well with clay, and expose to gentle heat for ten days, to accomplish extraction : decant the pure and clear extract thus obtained, free it by filtration from all fæcal impurities, place in glass vessel, and remove all the aqua fortis by distillation in the ashes. There will then remain at the bottom a dry, yellow powder of Antimony : pour on it distilled rain water, expose in similar glass vessel to moderate heat, and you will have a red tincture (or extract); filter, distil the rain water gently in S. Mary's Bath, and there will remain a red powder. Pour on it strong distilled vinegar, which, in time, is coloured red, like blood, and deposits a sediment. Distil this vinegar again, and again there remains a red powder. Reverberate this powder continuously for three days over an open fire, and extract from it the tincture with spirit of wine; then strain off the sediment that remains from the Tincture.

Again remove by distillation the spirit of wine (by S. Mary's Bath), and there will remain a fixed red powder of wondrous efficacy.* Half a drachm should be taken thrice daily, in the morning, at noon, and in the evening. It cleanses all ulcers, radically cures the French disease (syphilis), and renovates the whole frame.

It is now desirable that I should proceed to describe the preparation of the Flowers of Antimony, which is performed in various manners.†

---

* This is not the fixed Antimony sold by apothecaries : no, our fixed red powder is not to be bought either with silver or with gold, seeing that it is infinitely more precious than either. Let him that has this fixed powder use it in chronic diseases, especially where it is important to excite perspiration, and he will see the most wonderful effects.

† From the following pages, as from all contemporary literature, you may see in what evil repute the Art of

Of these flowers of Antimony the
world knows little or nothing, and it
will not be able to appreciate my pre-
scription. The students and friends of
this Spagyric Art, on the other hand,
will estimate it at its right value.
Nevertheless, I warn you, my disciples,
that if you desire to be true and earnest
Alchemists, you must take your cross
upon you, and follow me. You must
learn, as I have learned, to suffer, to
submit to persecution, to knock at the

Alchemy was held in the time of Basilius, and how many
theological and political authorities were to be found in the
army of ignorance arrayed against it. Now, you should
understand that I do not blame these writers for visiting
with the most severe invective those mountebank quacks
who practised their criminal intrigues under the cloak of
this Art. Such persons I consider as deserving not only
emphatic censure, but the most severe punishment. But
men of education and piety should not have been so blind
as to confound the innocent with the guilty, and to involve
honest Alchemists in one sweeping condemnation with these
charlatans. In our times the dense cloud of ignorance is
here and there shot with light ; physicians do not venture to
condemn Alchemy, and even prescribe Alchemistic remedies.
When will the darkness be utterly dispersed by the advent
of the Artist Elias, which Paracelsus predicts in some of his
books, as, for instance, in the 8th chapter of his treatise *De
Mineralibus:* "The common things God permits us to
make known, but the more momentous secrets cannot

gate of God's mercy without ceasing,
and to work patiently and unweariedly.
Then God will never leave you nor
forsake you, as He has never forsaken
me. But as to the flowers of Antimony,
you should learn that they may be
prepared in different ways, which all
students of Alchemy know. Some mix
them with salt ammonia, drive them
through the retort, and then wash out
the ammonia. These flowers are of a
beautiful white colour. Others sublime

---

become public property till the coming of the Artist Elias."
And to the same notion he gives expression in another place
(*Lib. Min. Tract. I.*) : " It is indeed true that many things
still remain hidden in the earth of which I, as well as others,
am ignorant. But this I know, that God will successively
reveal many marvels, and will bring to light many more
things than have hitherto been known to us all. This is
true—there is nothing hidden which shall not be uncovered.
After me there shall come one, whose equal does not live, and
who shall reveal many things." Therefore take heart, good
student of Alchemy, and prepare the way of Elias, who will
reveal more than has ever been known on earth before,
because of the wickedness of men. Give to the world as
much of this medicine of truth as, in its present condition,
it can assimilate, in order that it may gradually get well,
and be prepared for the times of Elias. " For the arts,"
adds Theophrastus, " equally possess their Elias, and it is
understood of the rest."

them over a strong fire, and, by placing three alembics on each other, they manage to prepare white, yellow, and red flowers at the same time. I have tried these ways, and find them useful ; but the most potent and efficacious flowers of Antimony are prepared as follows : Mix red flowers of Antimony with colcotar of vitriol, and sublime the mixture thrice. Then the essence of vitriol ascends with the flowers, and they become more effectual. Extract the flowers with spirit of wine, remove sediment, distil spirit of wine in Bath of S. Mary, till there remains a dry powder, which represents the purified flowers of Antimony. These I have shewn to the other friars, and to many who have consulted me in their spiritual and physical difficulties.

These flowers act as a gentle purgative ; they cure tertian and quartan fever, and most other diseases, so much so that I have determined, by the help of my Saviour Jesus and the most holy Mary, His Mother, to bequeath in my

will to suffering humanity all the remedies which I have extracted from the
bowels of the earth. The sublimed
Antimony, called flowers of Antimony,
is like the springs which well forth on
high mountains. Water is found both
by digging in the deep places of the
earth, and it rushes forth with great
force on the summits of high mountains.
How is this most remarkable fact to be
explained? I believe that the womb of
waters in the earth is more copiously
stored in some places than in others, so
that while you have to dig for water in
certain districts, in others, owing no
doubt to sidereal influences, it is drawn
upward with great force to the snowy
summits of the Alps, and to the pin-
nacles of the Tower of Babylon.* If
any foolish person should read these

---

* This parable is so clear to those from whose eyes the
cataract has been removed, that to explain it would be like
lighting a candle at noonday. Those who do not understand it should ponder it again and again, and let that which
they read to-day explain the difficulties of yesterday, and the
studies of to morrow throw light on the uncertainties of to-
day.

words, he will think that I am either
mad or drunk with wine. Well, I shall
then only be subjected to the same
suspicion as the disciples of the Saviour.
The water which rises by sublimation to
the mountain tops is purer and more
wholesome than that which is found in
the bowels of the earth. But if it be
driven upward, the earth still remains to
the Sages, and the salt can be extracted
as a means of separating the good from
the evil, the pure from the impure, the
gross from the subtle, the medicine from
the poison. Just in the same way, we
sons of earth are laid in the earth, and
there putrefy and are corrupted, till at
the last we are sublimed by the fire and
heat of heaven, and are purged of all
our sins and impurities, and become sons
of God and heirs of eternal life.

Let no one be offended at this
comparison of earthly and temporal
sublimation to heavenly and spiritual
sublimation. What I say, I say ad-
visedly, and yet I know very well the
difference between black and white,

between the gloom of earth and the serene brightness of heaven. Let us, therefore, proceed to describe another preparation of Antimony. All the different extracts of Antimony exhibit the most striking diversity in their practical effects. Yet their substance is the same, and they all are produced from the same source. It follows that their practical difference is altogether due to their preparation.

For instance, whatever is extracted from Antimony, or from anything else, by means of spirit of wine, acts quite differently from that which is extracted by means of good vinegar. Extracts made by means of spirit of wine have a strongly purgative effect ; extracts due to vinegar are rather constipating, because the volatile is thereby fixed and solidified.

This is a great arcanum, and of much more profound application than the common herds, whether they be masters or slaves, learned or unlearned, will be disposed to think.

Extracts are made from Antimony

either by means of spirit of wine, or by means of vinegar. Extract of glass of Antimony purges when made in the former way ; but made in the latter way, it does not occasion purgative action, and rather the reverse. Such facts as these, with which I have dealt at some length in my other writings, should set thoughtful men meditating, and may open up to them the inmost shrine of philosophical knowledge.

First of all, it is wonderful that every extract made with spirit of wine should have purgative properties ; while an extract of glass of Antimony, first made with vinegar, and (after the purging away of the vinegar) extracted with spirit of wine, retains not a trace of its purgative properties, but cleanses the system by means of sweats and salivary excretion through the mouth, purifies the blood, cures pulmonary disease, re-lieves asthma, and the most inveterate coughs and colds ; and is a most ad-mirable medicine.

Another extract of Antimony is pre-

pared in the following way: Pulverize
crude Antimony, pour to it strong mineral vinegar, put in vessel, close well,
and expose to the gentle rays of the sun.
After some time the vinegar will assume
a blood-red colour. Filter the extract,
and distil again in an alembic; it will
then exhibit some admirable and beautiful colours.

This oil is red as blood, has a
considerable sediment, and is of the
greatest medicinal value, especially in
the cure of leprosy.* It heals the new

---

* How timid has the wickedness of his contemporaries
made our Valentine! He does not tell us that from this
oil is prepared the quintessence of all things, extolled by
Peter of Spain as the greatest secret of philosophy. He
speaks so obscurely here of this all-important matter that it
is clear he has only written it in order to let the initiated
see that he was acquainted with the mystery. But in order
that you may not have spent your money in vain in buying
this book, and your time in reading it, I will give you clear
and straightforward directions which you must take care to
follow out in every particular. Take best friable Antimony,
for the crude kind, in spite of the advice of Basilius, is of
no use, because in its first distillation it has been deprived of
its most subtle sulphur; pulverise finely, pass through fine
sieve, place in broad-bottomed distilling vessel *(cucurbita)*,
add vinegar, distilled from its own proper minera, digest for
forty days. The vinegar will then be tinged, as it were, with

K

disease which has only recently made its appearance among our soldiers (venereal disease), and utterly consumes all morbific matter. Hence the physician should not grudge the time and trouble which must be given to the preparation of this Remedy.

Another extract of Antimony is prepared as follows : In the name of the Lord, take Antimony and crude tartar in equal parts, pulverize well together, place in strong crucible, which will not let the spirits escape ; calcine the substances in

---

blood. Pour this red Tincture into a retort, gently remove the vinegar by distillation. Make an extract of the powder which remains with spirit of wine, which will be of a blood-red colour. Pour into a circulatory vessel, like that represented on page 131, which is the most suitable I have met with for the volatilisation of substances. Digest the extract in S. Mary's Bath, till you see the tincture rise upward, and pass in a volatile state through the alembic. Let it cool. Place the whole substance in a glass cucurbit, distil the spirit according to art, and when it passes through the alembic it will be of a blood-red colour. Remove the spirit of wine, and you will have a thick, heavy oil. How this oil is united with its salt, and is then most valuable for the amelioration of metals, I will tell you in another place. In the meantime you may use the oil as a most efficacious Medicine, which prevails in desperate cases, accomplishing its purpose by profuse sweating.

Circulatory Vessel
for the
Volatilisation of Substances

a wind furnace till the tartar is entirely
burned; pulverize the burnt substance,
pour over it common hot water, and
cleanse and sweeten the substance with
lye. It will then become a "liver"
(hepar), a name given to it by the
ancients.* Dry this "liver," place it in
a cucurbit, add pure spirit of wine, extract the spirit by distillation in S.
Mary's Bath, so that a third part of it
remains. (First strain the spirit, etc.,
through a piece of paper.) This extract
should be used with great caution. It is

---

* The liver is a thing highly esteemed by gourmands,
and so is liver of Antimony among Alchemists. The operation is greatly improved by substituting salt of tartar for
plain tartar. Nor does Basilius tell us that the mortar in
which they are pounded must be hot; also he forgets to
specify the quantity of the water in which the powder must
be dissolved that it may assume a more beautiful colour.
Now, in this exaltation of colour there is a great inhering
virtue. Further, he omits to say that the precipitation of
the "liver" in the water takes place by means of vinegar.
Moreover, this fusion of Antimony, like all such fusions,
must be carried out on a bright sunny day. For, if you
laugh at me when I affirm that the heavenly bodies have
an important influence on the operations of the Alchemist,
I also will laugh at you when your experiments come to
nought. I know better than to waste any elaborate refu-
tation on those who make our Art and its claims the subject

a remarkable fact that the spirit of wine thenceforward refuses to mingle with the red extract whence it is derived, but floats on it, like oil upon water. But if the tincture of spirit of wine be poured on the liver of Antimony, it will attract it, yet the two will not amalgamate with the first extract. Who can declare all the wonders of God? Or who can rightly value the gifts which He has implanted in His creatures?*

I have spoken of the extract made from glass of Antimony by means of

---

of their scorn. For we speak of what we have seen with our eyes, and handled with our hands—but those ignorant persons suppose that they can establish a claim to wisdom by sneering at that of which they can know nothing. True lovers of Alchemy refuse to cast their pearls before swine. I affirm, then, that at certain seasons of the year, the liver of Antimony has a deeper colour and greater efficacy than that prepared at other times, its curative potency being greater both with regard to metals and to human bodies. As to the virtues of this medicine, there is no need of any elaborate recommendation. Everyone who has tried it knows its value, and is ready to exchange for it its weight in gold.

* In the following passage the Author speaks like a faithful teacher, who again and again inculcates the same truths upon the minds of his disciples. Yet he says that he does not use a single word too many, and therefore it will be well for you to keep your eyes open, and to listen with both your ears.

vinegar, and also by means of spirit of wine. Now I say that when this extract has been made with vinegar, and the vinegar removed (in S. Mary's Bath), the powder which remains is dissolved in a moist place into a yellow liquid. This liquid is wonderfully effective in the cure of old and fresh wounds, and my hand would weary of holding my pen if I attempted to set forth all its virtues. The same efficacy belongs to an extract from this powder before the solution with spirit of wine has been made. In the matter of internal disorders, it yields nothing to other medicaments.

I have described this preparation at some length in this treatise on Antimony, as well as in my other writings, because I know its value ; and I, therefore, trust and hope that my readers will not think the apparent repetitions in my books tedious. For though I may seem to repeat myself, I can assure you that I do not write a single word which does not demand the most careful attention on the part of the reader. Children and fools suppose that all is easy, because they do not understand it—but my true disciples will in course of time, and by dint of steady thought, apprehend my meaning.

Another extract is obtained by means of caustic water in the following manner : Take equal parts of vitriol and of common salt ; from these distil a water through the side.* The product, after violent heat, is a substance like melted butter, or olive oil. Reserve it for use. Pulverize the *caput mortuum* very finely, dissolve in water, strain through paper ; take Hungarian Antimony, pulverize finely, place in broad-bottomed cucurbit, add to it water, and subject to heat. After remaining there for a certain time, it becomes like an amethyst, of a dark violet ; increase the heat of the fire till

---

* I will tell you how to do this, in order to avoid bursting your vessels, during the distillation of the spirits of metals. Put the substance into an earthen retort A, through opening B, but gradually ; close up the opening ; the spirits then pass into recipient C, thence through D into recipient E, and thence again into receiver F ; the grosser spirits (G) remain at the bottom of receiver C, the more subtle spirits settle at the bottom of receiver F. See page 136.

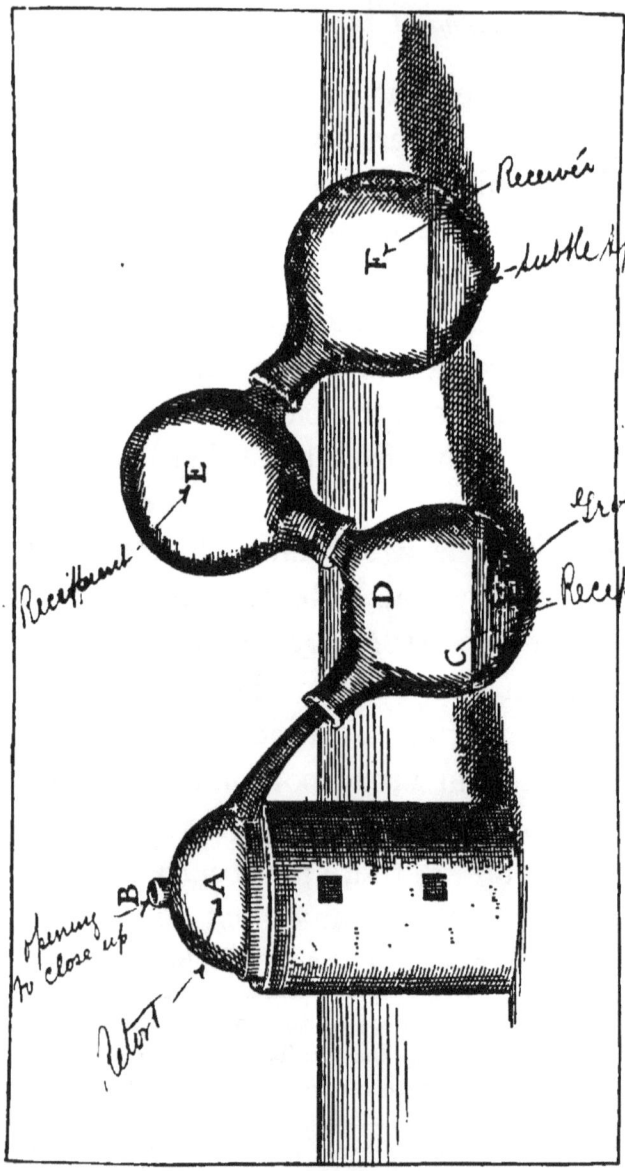

Receiver

subtle spirits

Grosser S[?]

Recipient

Recipient

E

D

F

G

A

B

opening
to close up

Retort

the substance becomes blue like a sapphire; from this is precipitated a white powder by the effusion of common water. This powder is an emetic and purgative like the red extract of glass of Antimony. In the first solution made of the *caput mortuum*, you may subject thin plates of iron to coction, and will then truly transmute Mars into Venus, as experience shews us. Again take the distilled oil or water before mentioned, pour over it crocus of Mars, reverberate with sulphur until it becomes red, expose to heat, and the tincture of iron, like blood, will be extracted. Take one part of this extract and three parts of the red extract of Antimony, which was prepared with burnt saltpetre and spirit of wine.*

---

* In the next sentence Basilius asks us to use water of Mercury, whose preparation he describes in the tract called Supplement. Moreover, there must be an opening in the retort, through which the water of Mercury is gradually poured in. If you put in too much of the Mercury at once, it may burst and overturn the retort and the furnace as well; hence you should have a succession of retorts (as on page 136) all in communication with each other. But as every true chemist is familiar with the potency of this Mercury in the resolution of metals, I will not enlarge on this point.

Inject gradually, by means of a long tube, one part of water of Mercury ; add half-a-part of calx of gold dissolved in caustic water ; distil all together over a gentle fire, and there will remain at the bottom a beautiful fixed solution.* The sanative virtues of this fixed solution are great, especially in the cure of open wounds. From the dead body which remains is prepared a solvent far more acrid than the strongest aqua fortis. The white powder is prepared from Antimony in the following way : Pulverize pure Hungarian Antimony, and an equal quantity of thrice-purified saltpetre ; burn this

---

* This solution is not yet fixed, but may become so by dint of patient work. Its chief use, which Basil does not even allude to, consists in the perfection of metals. For this purpose an extract must be made from the powder with strongest vinegar ; remove vinegar by distillation, sweeten what remains at the bottom with distilled water ; make a second extract with spirit of wine, abstract spirit ; the red powder which remains should be mixed with fixed salt prepared from the sediment which remained after the removal of the vinegar. After three months they should become fixed, and able to remain unchanged in the fire, as in their own proper element. When you have done this, you have made the fixed volatile, and the volatile fixed, and are not far from the fulfilment of your heart's desire.

composition all together in a new glazed pot, which is free from all grease, over a circulatory fire, but not all at once. (This operation the ancients called detonation.) Then pulverize the hard matter which remains in the pot; pour over it moderately hot ordinary water, and when the powder has settled at the bottom, add more water, till all the saltpetre is extracted.* Dry the substance, and again add to it its own weight of saltpetre; burn again, and repeat this operation three times; pulverize what then remains, add best spirit of wine, circulate diligently for a month in a well-closed cucurbit or circulatorium; pour to it, and remove, spirit of wine nine or ten times. Gently dry

---

* At this stage the substance is the powder of Ruland, with which he performed so many medicinal miracles. It should be prepared under a certain heavenly conjunction, and is the better the redder it is : for its colour is its soul. This is the true "crocus of metals," though not like the emetic which is sold under that name in shops. Take 8, 9, 10, or 11 grains of this powder, according to the strength of the patient; pour on them 3 or 4 oz. of wine; distil for four or five hours; the tincture of crocus of metals which is then extracted, is like blood ; give it to the patient as a gentle purgative : it will radically cure any disease in the treatment of which it may be employed.

powder ; heat for a whole day in crucible, such as is used by goldsmiths for the melting of silver and gold ; dissolve powder in a humid place, on a stone table, or in a hard-boiled egg. Dry the liquid which results, and restore to a pulverized condition.* The medicinal efficacy of this powder is great, but it requires time for its operation. If a man suffers from an internal tumour and takes a quarter of a drachm of this white fixed powder of Antimony in generous wine, five or six times, the tumour will be emptied of its corrupted blood without any prejudice to vital processes. It also consumes the new soldier's (venereal) disease, and expels it from the body. It renews the hair and the whole frame, invigorates the blood, and does more good than I am able to describe.

It would not be right for me to set down the whole of this Art so plainly and clearly that any one, even the most

---

* If you have experienced the virtues of the detonated powder, you will not be a Thomas as to the potency of this powder, which has been thrice detonated.

ignorant, might, on its perusal, become a perfect adept ; just as it is not well for a country bumpkin to eat the finest baker's bread.*

If any one should marvel because my book describes some operations which apparently differ from those of other Sages, let him know that the style of the Sages exhibits many important points of difference from that of other writers. You must not, therefore, quarrel with me : for I only adopt the necessary rules laid down by the ancient Masters of our Art.

The balm of Antimony is prepared, not of crude Antimony, but of the Regulus of Antimony, whence the living Mercury of Antimony is derived, and in the following manner.

---

* Yet Valentine has revealed the secrets of this Art more clearly than his successors, who have been busily employed in obscuring his light. Hence they do not praise him in the market place, though they esteem him most highly in the laboratory ; and they do not translate him into other tongues, though he is worthier than any other to speak all the languages of the world. But, of course, Basilius cannot describe the Art so clearly that any one, on taking up the book in an idle moment, may at once become a master of our noble Magistery.

Take equal parts of best Hungarian Antimony and crude tartar, and half the quantity of saltpetre ; pound together, melt over wind fire, pour into copper dish, allow to cool, and you will find the Regulus.* The Regulus is thrice, or oftener, purified with tartar and saltpetre till it becomes of a brilliant silvery white. Pulverise finely, place in vessel, add oil of juniper, or spirit of terebinth, which must have been previously distilled and must be pure as spring water ; digest in closed vessel in S. Mary's Bath ; the oil of juniper, or spirit of terebinth, will become red, like blood ; pour it out, and rectify with spirit of wine. The virtues of this balm of Antimony are the same as those of spirit of sulphur, which I will describe hereafter.

---

* As in the preparation of liver of Antimony, so here, you should take salt of tartar instead of crude tartar. The sal nitri is useless in this operation. Do not throw away the glassy substance ; for from it an useful cordial (dose 30 to 50 drops twice or thrice a day, in a suitable liquid) may be prepared by pounding it in a hot mortar, protecting it well from the moisture of the air ; place it in a vial, extract its tincture with alcohol of wine : it will be of a beautiful red colour.

Three drops of this balm, taken thrice a week in warm wine, cure pulmonary complaints, coughs, colds, and asthma.

Many other oils are prepared from Antimony, some simple and some compound. But the effects of all are different according to the difference in the method of their preparation. This fact may be illustrated in the following way. There are many living beings which dwell in and on the earth ; many have their abode in the air, many in the water, and some in the fire, like the salamander. Moreover, there are in tropical climes other animals of which we know nothing, except that they can live only in the warmth of the sun. In the same way, Antimony assumes a different nature according as it is prepared with water or with fire, only fire is in all cases indispensable. Again, the addition of earth produces a totally different compound to that produced by the addition of water ; and the result is quite different, again, when Antimony is sublimed in the fire.

The way of preparing simple uncompounded oil of Antimony, and true sulphur, is as follows : Place pulverised Hungarian Antimony in a glass cucurbit ; add true vinegar of the Sages, rendered more acid by means of its salt. Close the cucurbit, plunge it in horse dung, or S. Mary's Bath, for forty days, till the matter putrefies and the vinegar turns a deep red. Decant this vinegar, and keep adding more till no more red colour can be extracted. Strain off all the vinegar, pour into a clean vessel, plunge in horse dung, and allow to putrefy for forty days. Then the body is again dissolved, and the substance becomes as black as ink. This is the sign that the true solution has taken place, which will ultimately effect the separation of the elements.

Place this black substance into another cucurbit, and on an alembic ; distil the vinegar over a moderate fire, and it will rise as a clear fluid, while there remains at the bottom a dirty substance. Pulverise this, sweeten with distilled rain water, dry gently, and place in a long-necked circulatory vessel. The circulatory vessel should resemble three hollow balls placed one on the other, and communicating by means of tubes with a long neck at the top. Add highly rectified spirit of wine, so that it covers the substance to a height of two or three inches ; close the vessel well, and expose to gentle heat for two months, when the spirit of wine will become of a bright red ; pour out the extract, filter, place in a cucurbit, and remove the black sediment, which is of no further use to us.

Place the alembic on the cucurbit, and distil gently ; the spirit of wine will carry the tincture of Antimony upward, the elements are separated, and the alembic and receiver present the aspect of bright gold. Finally, some few dregs remain, but the gold colour in the glass utterly perishes. Place the red substance, which by distillation has passed into the receiver, in a circulatory vessel for ten days. By means of this circulation separation takes place ; for the oil has thereby acquired gravity, and sinks to the bottom, while the spirit of wine is limpid, as at first, and floats above the oil. Then separate the oil from the spirit in a separatory vessel.* This oil is of remarkable sweetness, most pleasant to use, and free from all corrosiveness.

No one can understand or comprehend the incredible virtue and potency of this Royal Oil. I call it the Balm of Life, because it can help, by the grace of God, those whom all physicians have given up. It renews a man's system just as if he were born again, purifies the blood, and, in conjunction with tincture of corals, casts out leprosy, drives away melancholy and sadness, braces up

---

* This is the substance of which all the Sages and Alchemists have written. This is the goal of all Alchemists, the oil of Antimony, which is soon to be converted into the Fire Stone. It is a Proteus which appears to us under different forms, and yet is ever the same. If you put together all the different operations which have been described, and regard them in the light of my commentary, you will have all the parts of the process by which our Stone is evolved; you will make the volatile fixed, and the fixed volatile, and then you have the great treasure coveted by the multitude. If you do not understand me, three shiploads of hellebore will not cure your folly.

the joints and the heart, improves the memory, and is our great sheet-anchor in consumption.

But why should I continue to enumerate the blessed virtues of this Oil? Few indeed of our doctors and medical magnificoes will credit a tittle of what I say. Those, on the other hand, who have experienced the magical potency of our Medicine, and do listen to my teaching, will believe me without much praise and recommendation, nay, will bless my memory when I am mouldering in the grave. Another way in which this Oil may be prepared, is as follows :

Place Regulus of Antimony, well pulverised, in a great round glass vessel, over a gentle fire in the sand. Brush off all that is sublimed, so that it falls down again to the bottom, and continue to do this till no further sublimation takes place, but the whole substance remains at the bottom. Then the Regulus of Antimony has been fixed without any addition. But, in order to bring about this result, you need patience. Pulverize the red precipitate, place on a smooth, clean stone in a humid cave ; leave it there six months, till the precipitate resolves itself into a pure red liquid, and a sediment is separated from it, *i.e.*, the salt of Antimony only is dissolved. Filter the liquid, place in cucurbit, extract phlegm, place again in the cave, and it will crystallize beautifully ; separate from the phlegm ; the crystals are pellucid, mixed with red colour. When they are again purified, they become white.* Dry this Salt of Antimony, mix with it three parts of Venetian earth (called tripel), and distil over strong fire. There will be sublimed first a white and then a red spirit, which also becomes white. Rectify gently in a dry bath, and you have another white oil distilled from Antimony, but it is by no means so good as the former salt made of the red Tincture.

This spirit, or salt, distilled after a spiritual manner, is useful in quartan

---

* "Like to like" is a Greek proverb, and certainly this salt is more effectual in making extracts from Antimony than even from other metals.

fever, and in the breaking up of vesical stones, as also in gout ; it purifies wounds inflicted with iron, and the blood generally. Yet it is not as perfect in its operation as the red oil of Antimony, the sulphur of which is highly and perfectly digested.

I have spoken of the salt and sulphur of Antimony, and have described their medicinal uses ; I now proceed to discuss the medicine, which is profoundly hidden in its Mercury.

Take eight parts of Regulus of Antimony, one part of salt clarified and sublimed from human urine, one part of sal ammoniac, and one of salt of tartar ; mix well in vessel, add strong vinegar, and close up with the clay of the Sages ; digest the salts with vinegar a whole month over a suitable fire. Put all into a cucurbit and distil vinegar in ashes. Mix to salts, thus dried, three parts of Venetian earth ; distil with strong fire through the retort, and you have a marvellous spirit, which add to the pulverized Regulus of Antimony ; let

them putrefy two months, then distil
vinegar gently, and mix with that which
remains a fourfold weight of steel filings ;
distil over a strong fire through the
retort ; the spirit of salt will then carry
the Mercury with it in form of smoke ;
let it be driven into a large glass receiver
full of water : the spirit of salt then
mingles with the water, but the Mercury
is precipitated to the bottom, as true
Mercury.* This is the way in which
running Mercury is prepared from Antimony : we must now go on to describe
its uses.

Take, in the name of the Lord, one
part of this Mercury, and strain it
through leather ; take four parts of
highly rectified oil of red vitriol ; extract

---

* Certain secrets which were deeply concealed in the
days of Basilius are now included among the common processes of chemists No person could now be regarded as a
true chemist who is ignorant of the method by which Mercury is composed out of Antimony, whether that which
Basilius teaches, or another method, for various artists have
excogitated various ways, and that which has been successfully proved by one is by him favoured in proportion. How
many Alchemists in those times could elicit the Mercury of
Antimony ? Yet they looked down on Basilius, forsooth, and
upon his whole system.

the oil, when there will remain its spirit, with the Mercury ; sublime over a strong fire, and place all that is sublimed again at the bottom of the vessel. Pour to it as much of the oil of vitriol as before, and repeat the process three times. At the fourth time place all that is sublimed with the sediment ; pound, and it will be pure and bright as crystal ; place in cir- culatory vessel, add the same quantity of oil of vitriol, and three times as much spirit of wine ; circulate till separation takes place, and the Mercury is resolved into oil, floating over the rest like olive oil. Separate this oil from the re- mainder, place in circulatory vessel, pour to it strong distilled vinegar, and leave for twenty days ; hereby the oil recovers its gravity, and drops to the bottom, while all that was poisonous in it remains in the vinegar.*

---

* No candle is needed at midday, nor need the com- mentator speak when the author is so clear and lucid. Only go forward bravely, planting your feet firmly at every step, and you will at last obtain the golden branch. For this oil itself possesses marvellous efficacy in the improvement of metals, and yields only to the King of Kings himself.

This is that great wonder, by which the oil first floats, and then becomes heavy and sinks to the bottom. Observe that the oil of vitriol is also heavy, but at first the Mercury is rendered lighter by the impurities which still adhere to it ; subsequently those impurities remain in the vinegar ; the Mercury recovers its proper gravity, and is precipitated to the bottom. This oil of Mercury is the fourth pillar of Medicine. It stimulates the vital action of the brain, makes men active, and cures both leprosy and paralysis. If any one who has been suffering from chronic disease uses this oil daily for some time, his nails and hair drop off and grow again, his whole frame is rapidly renovated, his blood purified, and all morbid matter expelled. The French disease is easily and radically cured by this remedy.

Let us, then, thank God from the bottom of our hearts for this Medicine which He has so graciously bestowed upon us ! And you, Doctors and Surgeons, you I exhort to come to me, a

monk, and servant of God, and I will
shew you what your eyes have never
seen ; I will point out to you the way of
health, along which you have never led
your patients. If any one should understand this Art better than myself, let
him not be silent, nor attach a padlock
to his lips. I shall not be ashamed to
learn of him. I have often said that our
life is too short for one man to investigate all the mysteries of knowledge. On
the other hand, let those be silent who
know less than I, who also do not even
understand my books ; let them refrain
from hasty reprehension, and from teaching their schoolmaster the alphabet.

My terminology has a different
sound and a different meaning from that
of my opponents, who are too lazy and
indolent to plant and graft trees, and,
therefore, never get beyond their wilding
plants or withered branches carelessly
stuck in the ground.

Be not over hasty in judging and
condemning that of which you know
absolutely nothing. You may be one of

those who suppose, with the multitude, that in winter fishes are frozen to death in the water. But that is a notion in support of which not a tittle of evidence has ever been produced.

The reason that fishes sometimes die in the winter is to be sought in the fact that no animal can live without air, and when the ice is frozen over the fish are frequently suffocated. Now, if Antimony is to bear its own proper fruit, it must not be suffocated in the bowels of the earth ; but it must be dug out, and prepared by the auxiliary media of water, air, and fire, lest its fruitfulness be strangled in the earth. It must be made manifest by many laborious preparations of the artist, in order that it may be effectual for the healing of diseases and for the perfecting of metals.

What, then, can you say, or what argument can you bring forward that is of the slightest weight? Since you are so densely ignorant as to have not even the slightest idea of the composition of Antimony, you do well to keep your own counsel, and to suffer this tempest of rebuke and censure to sweep over your bowed head, lest you suffer shipwreck of reputation as well as of knowledge.

In order that you may escape this danger, call at once upon your sleeping Master, as the disciples of Jesus called upon their Lord while He slept; invoke Him with an unfeigned heart, and you will be helped, and will see the wind and waves obedient to His Word, while your undertaking will be brought to its desired close. If men would only be more earnest in their endeavour to know the truth, God would then give them grace and wisdom, and they would in due time find the precious corner-stone on which the whole structure rests. Then the ears of students in the schools, and the heads of patients in sick-rooms, would no longer be tormented with the absurdities of the old system of medicine. The stone-built citadel of our Art cannot be so quickly destroyed by fire as a dovecote or a stork's nest made of rotten wood, and dried day after day by the sun.

But you who are true disciples of
this Art, strive to penetrate to its centre;
be not content to linger on the surface.
Pursue your object as the hunter pursues
the quarry, and take care that you do
not catch a hind for a buck, or a fox for
a hare. Cast your nets well, and you
will enclose a great multitude of .fishes ;
lay your traps discreetly, and the birds
will not escape. Let the fowler place
his snares with due regard to the wind ;
let the mariner, who is driven hither and
thither by the tempestuous heavings of
the vast ocean, look well to his compass,
and then his ship will surely return with
a rich cargo of merchandise.

But why do I waste my time, like
those empty-headed boasters, in treading
out straw ? Nay, but I am not threshing
empty straw, for there is not a single
word in my books that is without its
significance and utility.

Now I will fall back one step, like
the gladiators, and introduce a new subject, viz., the way in which Antimony
should be prepared for the treatment of

external wounds. I have already briefly described the preparations which are most useful from a medical point of view; I will next mention some other preparations which will one day revolutionize the Art of the surgeon.

Young man, you who desire to know the secret things of Nature, and to bring to light her hidden mysteries, listen to me, that you may be able to distinguish day from night, and the clear from the obscure. Take one part of Hungarian Antimony, half a part of common salt, six parts of unburned clay ; pound together and distil vehemently, without intermission, till the oil passes upward ; then remove its thickness by distillation, so that a red dry powder remains at the bottom of the cucurbit ; pulverize, dissolve on a slab of marble, and you have a red, brilliant balm for wounds, which far excels all other similar remedies. Its utility is great in the case of wounds which have been open for a long time.*

---

* A prudent general so arrays his forces as to place the good soldiers in the front ranks, the best in the rear, and

The open wounds, in the treatment of which this balm produces striking results, are especially those on which the medical profession have brought their plasters, ligaments, and ointments to bear in vain.

You see that I speak out with great simplicity, for I am a monk, and know not the ways of the world. Yet I cannot always discourse so plainly and lucidly as the nature of the subject would seem to require.

This oil is very helpful in serious cases of accident, and more especially in old wounds, so that few medicines can surpass it. That oil which is prepared with the common sublimate of the apothecaries has equal efficacy, and, frequently, as experience has taught, is superior in cancer, lupus, and similar complaints. But in ordinary cases of fistula, and in bruises and ruptures, this balm has great efficacy. I do not mention all its marvellous effects,

---

those that are less good and brave in the middle. The orator arranges his arguments on the same principle, and Basilius follows their precedent.

which only experience can prove, lest I should be thought to be excited by ambition, or by desire for fame. I declare I have sought or desired neither. I deny that either can be sought with righteousness. The other oil is prepared in the following manner :

Take mortified Mercury, sublimed into a state of great brilliancy (this may be bought at the apothecary's), and Antimony in equal parts ; pulverize together, distil thrice out of a retort which retains the spirits, rectify the oil with spirit of wine, and your oil will be of a blood-red colour. At first, however, it is white like ice, or coagulated butter. This oil exhibits its efficacy in all desperate cases, and especially in the perfect emendation of the evil into good.

By means of an addition, you may also prepare another oil for external wounds, which will be of palmary utility. It is composed in the following manner :

Take one part of Antimony, one of sulphur, half a part of salt ammoniac, or purified salt of urine, and two parts of quicklime. Expel the oil strongly, pound all that is sublimed with the dead body, pour to it oil a second time, distil thrice, and the oil is prepared.

In cases where old wounds resist all other remedies. you may use this oil. For it is strong, potent, and penetrative, and lays a good foundation for other medicines.

An admirable balm for old wounds is prepared with various ingredients in the following manner :

Digest four ounces of sulphur and half a pound of Mercury over a moderate fire, stirring with a wooden spoon; pound fine till they form one solid mass (for it is made as cinnabar is usually prepared), and with it four ounces of Antimony, four ounces of red arsenic, and two ounces of "crocus of iron." * Place in glass cucurbit, and sublime. As the result of this operation you will have pyropus stones the colour of which is fully equal to those of the East, except that they are not fixed, and vanish in

---

* Sulphate of iron.

the fire. In order that the artist may separate the pyropus stones from the cinnabar, which during sublimation ascends, pulverize, and make an extract with strong distilled vinegar. Distil vinegar gradually in S. Mary's Bath, and there remains a powder ; further pulverize, place in another glass vessel, extract tincture with spirit of wine, and throw away the sediment. Digest the extract in a well-closed bath for a month, remove spirit of wine by distillation, place the remaining powder on a flat glass dish in a tub full of water, so that the plate floats on it like a boat ; in a few days the powder will resolve itself into a clear liquid.

This tincture is useful in the treatment of old open wounds, and is sure to be highly efficacious in cases where all other remedies have failed. Open ulcers which have their origin in internal conditions, must be treated internally, and thus radically extirpated. But ulcers caused by inflammation may be successfully cured with this Tincture.

M

If men would consider the mass of
suffering which the sin of our first parents
has brought upon our race, and the sorrow, disease, misery, and pain which have
followed in the train of that first fall, they
would be more industrious in seeking the
salvation of their neighbour, proffered at
so great a price by the Chief Ruler of
Heaven. But alas, great numbers of
men live on from day to day without thus
redeeming the time for the glory of God
and the good of their neighbours! They
are afraid, forsooth, of soiling the very
tips of their fingers, just as if they
grudged the grocer the profits which he
derives from the sale of soap. But do
we not all live in this world as the vas-
sals of God, and are not all our goods
His feudal possessions, granted to us
during life only? Let us, therefore,
make a good and kindly use of them in
order that we may be able to render a
joyful account in the presence of the
Great Master, instead of being, by reason
of our ingratitude, cast into outer darkness, where there is weeping and gnash-

ing of teeth. If all were inspired and actuated by this solemn thought, there would be less sin and more persevering effort for the good of the whole race. But for these things worldly men do not care. Their one desire and aim is gold, and only gold; the powerful seek to obtain it by violence, and the poor by crying servility—that they, too, may be partakers of the Mammon of iniquity.

But beware lest you be choked by the bone in your greedy throats, and lest the fish bones pierce your hearts! And you who will not listen to exhortation, hear a parable. When I was, in pursuance of a vow, performing a pilgrimage to San Jago, I prayed that God might grant me a safe return to our monastery. God answered my prayer, and I believed that my return would give great and sincere joy to all; for I brought back a large number of relics for the honour of our monastery, and the relief of the sick and poor. Yet I am afraid that few men derived wonderful benefit from these relics, or were grateful to God, but persisted in their mockery and scorn.

The following preparation of Antimony is useful against fevers and the plague itself, as I have myself experienced : Pulverize Antimony, place in a glass retort, distil over a strong fire three or four times ; let it be kept in a large vase till it becomes a red powder ; extract with vinegar, circulate, extract ten days over a gentle fire, remove vinegar by distillation, and transfuse what remains by a skilful process into an oil.*

Four grains of this oil, taken with St. Benedict's cordial, cures quotidian, tertian, and quartan fevers, if the patient be well covered and perspire freely. The same dose is an efficacious remedy against the plague, being mingled with spirit of wine or distilled vinegar, according as the disease first makes itself felt in an excess of heat or cold. Three friars in our monastery, who had already

---

* This extract must be made volatile with spirit of wine, as above. Let the humidity of the oil be removed by circulation, so that it becomes a dry powder.

made their wills, were thus restored, and
ever since that time their gratitude in-
duced them to take a great interest in
our Art, and to assist me as much as
they could during their spare time.
For all the help so kindly rendered to
me, I would have allotted to them a
prominent place in my last will, but
they have now gone to their rest before
me, and I commit them to the Great
Physician who is in heaven. May
He give them a good recompense of
joy which was denied them here on
earth !

Another oil, which is good for the
cure of wounds, is prepared from Antimony in the following manner : Take of
Antimony, sulphur, and saltpetre, equal
parts ; detonate under a bell, like the oil
of sulphur. This method of preparation
was early known to the Ancients. It is
better still to take an alembic instead of
the bell, and place near it a receiver ;
thus you obtain more oil, and of the
same colour as that extracted from
vulgar sulphur, but highly superior as to

its strength and efficacy.* We use three drops of this oil with the spirit of wine internally against pulmonary consumption ; used outwardly as a liniment, covered with a stiptic plaster, it is most efficacious in the treatment of foul or festering wounds and sores.

Another oil of Antimony for the cure of cancerous and corrosive wounds is prepared as follows : Pound together one pound of Antimony, half a pound of common salt, and five pounds of broken latera ; place in retort and distil a yellow oil, when all the spirits will pass away. Pour into fresh vessel, and remove its oiliness ; there remains a powder, which, spread on a stone, in a humid place, and you will have a humid balm which is of great efficacy against foul wounds, and cancer in the face, or when it attacks the breasts of women.

---

* If you use the vessel roughly sketched on page 167, you will get as much oil of sulphur from one ounce, as from a pound by the ordinary method, *i.e.*, from sixteen ounces of sulphur you wiil get half-an-ounce of oil, for which you would otherwise require sixteen pounds.

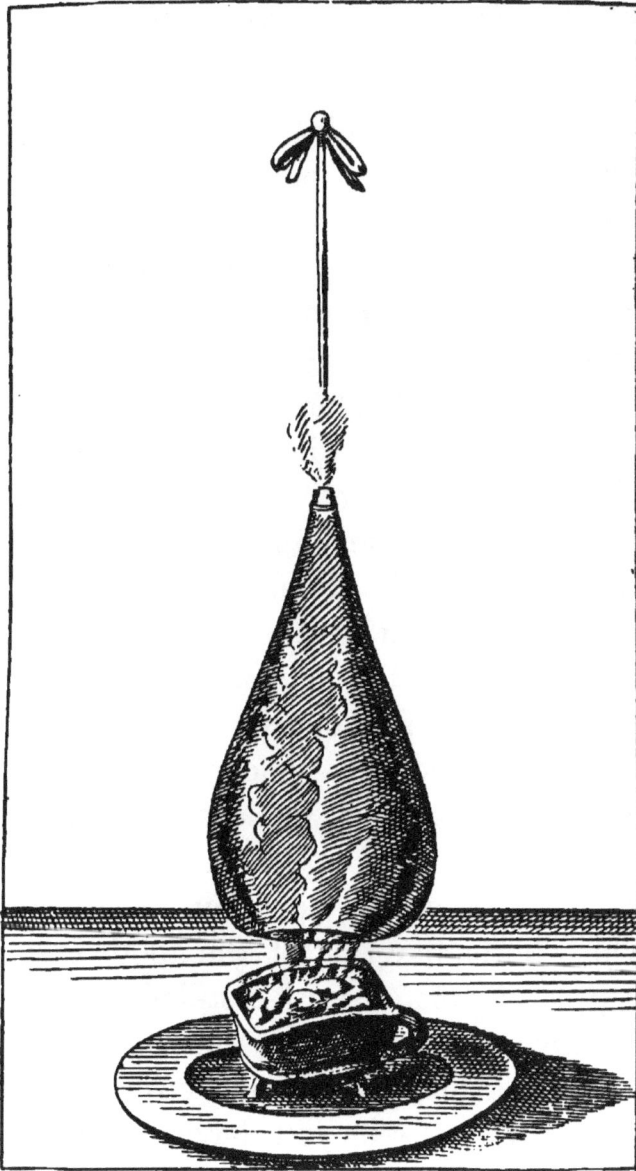

I would dilate still further on the virtues of this oil, only I am afraid that some foolish member of the profession may charge me with saying more than I know, and committing to paper mere wild speculations.

Another oil is prepared as follows : Let one part of Antimony be sublimed with a fourth part of salt armoniac. The salt raises the sulphur of Antimony to a bright red. Pound the sublimed substance, and if at the first you have taken one pound of Antimony, pound with it again five ounces of Antimony ; sublime as before ; and dissolve the sublimed substance in a moist place. Sweeten by removing the salt added to it ; dry gently, and you have a sulphur which burns like that of the apothecary. Extract its tincture with distilled vinegar. Remove vinegar gently in S. Mary's Bath, transtil the remaining powder very gradually, and—if you have made no mistake—you have an excellent oil, sweet, pleasant, and grateful in its use,

without any corrosivity or danger.*
There are other effects which this
Medicine has in common with other
preparations of Antimony, and, therefore, I do not enumerate them, in order
to give no occasion to the adversary, and
to avoid wearying the reader by repetition. The liquid, which is dissolved in
a moist place, is an external medicine,
and very useful in skin diseases. Mixed
with oil of tartar, and applied to a whit-
low, it produces marvellous effects ; it is
also of great utility in the treatment of
scrofula.

Sulphur of Antimony may also be
prepared in the following manner : Pulverize the Antimony, and digest for two

---

* This is another way of preparing the balm or quintessence of Antimony—for by that latter name Basilius
describes it in his other writings. There is, of course, a
difference, *e.g.*, here the separation is made with salt of
ammonia, and there it was made with vinegar. But even
these slight divergencies afford scope for the ingenuity of the
operator. This oil cures consumption and all pulmonary
complaints ; it relieves asthma and difficulty of breathing.
Take two grains in spirit of wine in the morning, and in the
evening, before retiring, in elixir or spirit of wine. It will
enlarge the chest, and purge out all phlegm and every
obstruction.

hours, or longer, in a strong lye made of
the ashes of beechwood. Strain, add
vinegar, and the sulphur will be of a red
colour, and sink to the bottom ; pour off
the liquid, and dry the powder gently.
Distil this powder with grape vinegar,
extract the tincture, and treat the sulphur
as in the last operation, *i.e.*, convert it
into oil by distillation. The sulphur
mentioned above has indeed greater
potency, because it was sublimated and
better dissolved at the beginning with
salt armoniac.

The other preparations of Antimony
which the Spagyrist should be able to
make, are the Vinegar of Antimony, the
Philosophical Signed Star, and the Lead
of the Sages, concerning which there has
been much vain speculation, it being said,
for instance, that genuine Mercury could
be prepared from it. But Mercury, as
the first substance or first water of the
metals, and the seed thereof, whence the
Stone of the Ancient Sages is evolved,
is not found in Antimony, but in another
mineral which has a more potent metallic

action than Antimony; yet Antimony
supplies a particular and most useful
operation. The Alchemist should know
exactly the uses of Antimony, both as an
external and internal medicine, and also
the distinctive aspects of Antimony as
compared with metals, for not until then
will he have a perfect judgment on these
points.

I will now proceed to satisfy my
disciples, and give them proper instruction how they are to separate the good
from the evil in the preparation of
vinegar from Antimony.

Pulverize ore of Antimony, place in
round glass vessel, with an oblong neck,
pour on it distilled rain water, so as to
half-fill the cucurbit; close well, and
plunge in horse dung for putrefaction, till
the ore begins to effervesce and deposit
a foam on the surface. Then it is time
to take it out, as it is a sign that the body
has opened. Place in another cucurbit, close well, and extract water, which
will have an acid taste. When all the
water is distilled, increase the heat, and

the substance will be sublimed. Pound again with the sediment and add the same water, and again extract, when it will already be much more acid. Repeat the operation till the water is as sour as ordinary vinegar. The oftener the process is repeated, the less there is of the sublimed substance. Pour this vinegar over some more of the raw ore to the height of about three inches. Digest in a pelican for twelve days, till the vinegar becomes red, and more acid than before. Decant and distil in S. Mary's Bath, without addition of anything; the clear vinegar will then rise, while the red powder remains at the bottom, and if an extract be made with spirit of wine, it is an excellent medicine. Rectify the vinegar once more in S. Mary's Bath, to free it from its phelgm. Dissolve in its own salt, *i.e.*, one ounce in four ounces; sublime in ashes, and the vinegar will be more acid, and acquire greater strength and efficacy.* This vinegar has a wonderful

---

* This vinegar is one of the principal preparations from Antimony, and therefore I subjoin the following par-

cooling effect, being far more potent in this respect than is ordinary vinegar ; it stops gangrene and heals cancerous wounds by outward application, if it be made into an ointment with Soul of Saturn. It also soothes and relieves inflammation, when mixed with endive water to which *sal prunellæ* has been added. The activity of inflamed blood is also soothed thereby. At the time of plague the vinegar (one spoonful) is a wonderful preventive, and extracts the poison from the boils, if applied as an ointment. For this purpose it should be

---

ticulars, which will enable you to carry out the directions of Basilius more perfectly. To six pounds of Antimony you require fourteen pounds of distilled water ; the success of the next distillation is ensured by placing the alembic so that its spout is immersed in water (see p. 174), else more than one-half of the spirit of Antimony will be lost. When, after the distillation of the water, the fire is quickened, you should keep it up for three days and three nights ; then let it cool, and mix that which is sublimed with fresh Antimony ; resume the process again for three days and three nights, and so a third time. If you convert the vinegar into a tincture with some more ore of Antimony, you will have the tincture which Basilius calls the balm of life. Did men only know the mysteries which lie concealed therein, I know not whether any other operation upon Antimony would be attempted. Verily, this contains them all.

mixed with a third part of water distilled from frog's spawn.

Many have esteemed the Signed Star of Antimony very highly, and spared neither labour nor expense to bring about its preparation. But very few have ever succeeded in realizing their wishes. Some have thought that this Star is the true substance of the Philosopher's Stone. But this is a mistaken notion, and those who entertain it stray far afield from the straight and royal road, and torment themselves with breaking rocks on which the eagles and the wild goats have fixed their abode. This Star is not so precious as to contain the Great Stone ; but yet there is hidden in it a wonderful medicine, which also may be prepared from it. The Star is compounded in the following way :

Take two parts of Hungarian Antimony, and one part of steel ; melt with four parts of burnt tartar in an iron basin, such as those in which goldsmiths refine gold. Cool, take out the Regulus, remove all impurities and scoriæ, pulverize finely, add to it, after ascertaining its weight, three times as much burnt tartar; melt, and pour into basin as before. Repeat a third time, and the Regulus becomes highly refined and brilliant. If you have performed the fusion properly —which is the point of greatest importance—you will have a beautiful star of a a brilliant white.* The Star is as distinct as if a draughtsman had traced it with a pair of compasses.

This star with salt armoniac is reduced to a red sublimate, for the tincture of iron ascends. This sublimate may be dissolved into a liquid of highly surgical utility.†

This Regulus, or Star, may be very often carried through the fire with a stone serpent, till at length it consumes itself, and is completely joined to the

---

* In the third fusion of the Regulus the fire should be most intense, so as to remove any remaining impurity.

† The said sublimate, before being placed in a cave for dissolution, should be purged of its salt armoniac with distilled water. For want of such trifling hints much labour and expense may often be vainly incurred.

serpent.* The Alchemist has then a hot
and ignitable substance, in which wonderful possibilities are latent. It is dissolved into an oil, which should be
purified and clarified by transfusion and
distillation. Three drops of this oil in
two ounces of wine may be administered
internally, but with great caution, and
not oftener than twice a week. The
proportion should be determined by the
peculiar circumstances of the disease,
which should, therefore, be known to the
physician.

This is a remarkable acrid substance, comprehending within itself
many arcana, but there is no need to
reveal everything at once to the ignorant.
Some Arts must be kept secret, in order
to stimulate the spirit of enquiry.† Whoever would follow in my footsteps should

---

* The serpent is that which mingles with the King,
and he calls it a serpent of stone, because it is a salt.

† Whoever understands the immense importance of
extracting essences from metals will value this acrid oil,
which is really the great metallic solvent, and without
which the entrance to the Great Arcanum, and to the
throne of the kingdom of chemistry, would be closed.

N

never grow weary in the search, but do in all things as I have done, and he will attain to the same result.

This is a book which sets forth the rudiments of the Art. Many spend their whole life in trying to master the elements, and never attain to the real objects of their search. In order to prevent the recurrence of such fruitless lives, I have here set down a full account of all that is necessary for the beginner to know.

In this oil wonderful effects lay hidden. For if circulated a long time, it finally forms into crystals, and after three days and three nights calcination there is elicited from them a salt; and then this oil is again distilled through the retort. In this way is prepared a medicine which dissolves vesical stones, and is of great efficacy in many other complaints.

As to the Lead of the Sages, let me tell the student that there exists a great affinity between common lead and Antimony. As some trees separate through their bark a certain resin or gum, like that of the cherry tree, for instance, which gum bears no manner of resemblance to the tree itself, or to its natural fruit, differing as it does from them in taste and in its other properties — so the earth brings forth certain abortions which are separated and purged off from the pure metals.

Though lead has a close affinity to Antimony, yet Antimony has been cast out by lead on account of its excess of sulphur, so that it could not bring its viscous body to perfection, and takes its place among the minerals. Its abundance of sulphur has hindered the coagulation of its Mercury, and thus prevented it from becoming a malleable body. There is no lead in Antimony but its Regulus, though this Regulus has not yet attained to its brilliancy, and though the Philosopher's Stone cannot be evolved from it. The reason why lead is called the Regulus, or King, is as follows : If the King which Antimony gives out in the preparation of glass be taken and placed in a fire-resisting and well-closed crucible, with salt of Saturn, and melted in a wind furnace till the Regulus is extracted, it is rendered more viscous and ponderous than before; for it has received ponderosity from the spirit of salt, and consistency as well, its body having become compact and heavy.* Hence I say that there is no very great difference between the Signed Star and the Lead of Antimony; for both are prepared from glass of Antimony, and their medicinal effects are the same. But now I will break off, and, after setting forth my appendix, I will explain the meaning and the nature of the Fire Stone.

Bestow upon us Thy blessing, O God, and open the hearts of my readers that they may see, know, and acknowledge Thy omnipotence and wonderful working in Nature, for Thy glory, and the healing of the sick! Amen.

---

* Let this Regulus, which is rendered malleable with salt of Saturn, be mixed with equal parts of Mercury, condensed with Saturn; let them be fused and well combined in a hot furnace, and you have a substance which in its outward appearance resembles silver, but in its properties is far more precious than silver. Hammer into thin plates, and apply to any inveterate wound, fistula, or ulcer, which has resisted all the plasters and ointments of the profession.

APPENDIX.

I N conclusion, you should know that Antimony is used for a good many purposes besides those of the typographer. Under a certain favourable stellar conjunction there are cast from it certain characters and amulets of great virtue and potency. In the same way metal mirrors may be prepared which possess all but magical properties. There are also founded from it bells of great sweetness of sound, images of men, and many other things besides.* But as these matters

---

* Without yielding to the temptation of taking up the lamentation of Basilius over the folly and carelessness of men, who are so engrossed with the greed of gold that they do not bestow much attention on the wonderful virtues which God has implanted in created things, let me at least make the following remark : Antimony is a mineral in which so wonderful a spirit is hidden, that its virtues are inexhaustible, and its powers transcend human knowledge. Nor do I

182 *The Triumphal Chariot of Antimony.*

have nothing to do with my vocation and calling in life, I leave them to those who can do them more justice than myself.

---

believe that in other things Antimony would possess less remarkable capabilities than in Alchemy and Medicine I will not tell you what I think of the characters and amulets which Basilius mentions ; but it is a fact that Antimony exhibits far more sympathetic affinity to the stars than any other metal or mineral.

On the Triumphal Chariot of Antimony, and the Nature of the Fire Stone.

BEING removed from all worldly care by the fervour of prayer and heavenly thoughts, I determined to yield up my soul to those spiritual inspirations without which it is impossible to have a right knowledge of created things. I proposed to furnish myself with wings wherewith I might ascend to the stars and inspect the heavens, as Icarus had done before me, if we may believe the old writers.*

But, when I approached the sun too closely, my feathers were consumed by

---

* We cannot wonder if here, where he has reached the climax of his work, and is about to explain the secret of secrets, Basilius hides his meaning from the foolish and the scornful under the guise of a parable. The true disciple of our Art will be all the more encouraged to press onward, and to remove the veil which hides the secret.

his burning heat, and I fell headlong into
the sea ; then, in answer to my prayer,
God sent an angel to help me, who bade
the waves be still, and caused a great
mountain to arise in the midst of the
water. I ascended it to see whether
there really existed that correspondence
between things below and things above
of which so much has been said, and
whether the stars possess the power of
producing things resembling them on
earth.* As the result of my investigation I found that what the ancient Doctors have delivered to their disciples was
God's own truth. Therefore I rendered
profound thanks to the Lord of Heaven
and earth for His wonderful works.

To put the matter briefly, I find
that all that is dug up from the bowels
of the mountains is infused by the stars
and celestial bodies, and derives its
origin from a certain aqueous vapour,
which, after being nourished by the
stars for a long time, is reduced to a

---

* This correspondence exists, and no one who has the
least Alchemistic experience can be disposed to deny it.

tangible shape by the elements. Further-
more, as the fire, with the aid of air,
gains the ascendency, that aqueous substance becomes dry; out of water is
produced fire, and out of fire and air we
obtain earth; all these elements are still
found in all bodies before their separation. Water, formed into earth by fire
and air, is thus the first substance of all
things.*

The Fire Stone which is prepared
from Antimony, which also I have
promised to describe, does not only cure
the diseases of men, but it removes the
imperfections of metals. I must proceed
to tell you what the Fire Stone is; what
is its ore; whether it can be prepared
without a proper substance; wherein
consists the difference of the stones;
how many kinds of them there are; and,
finally, what are their uses. May God

---

* This, as all Sages agree in telling us, is the substance
from which is prepared the lesser Fire Stone, and the Great
Stone of the Philosophers. It is the Water of Anaxagoras,
the Fire of Empedocles, the First Substance of Aristotle.
It is that by which trees grow, men are nourished, and
metals generated.

illumine my mind by His Holy Spirit that I may perform this task aright, and be able to appear before Him with a clear conscience on the day of judgment, when sentence will be pronounced upon the lives of all men !

Above everything you should know that the true tincture of Antimony, which is the Medicine of men and metals, is not prepared from crude, melted Antimony, which is bought in shops, but from the ore of Antimony, as it is dug up from the mine, and is first formed into glass. The great and im-· portant question is : How is this tincture extracted ? Know also that the prepared, fixed, and solid tincture of Antimony, or Fire Stone, as I prefer to name it, is a pure essence of penetrative, spiritual, and igneous quality, and is reduced into a coagulated substance, which, like the salamander, rejoices in the fire as in its own proper element.

But the Fire Stone is not an universal Tincture, like the Philosopher's Stone, which is prepared from the essence of gold.* Our Fire Stone tinges silver into gold, and also perfects tin and lead, but does not transmute iron and copper, nor does it impart to them more than can be obtained from them by separation. One part of this tincture has no power to transmute more than five parts of any imperfect metal. The great Philosopher's Stone, on the other hand, has infinite power of transmutation. Yet the precious metal produced by the Fire Stone is pure and solid gold.

The ore from which this tincture is prepared, is, as I have already stated, the earth of Antimony. In the meantime, let the reader observe that there are many kinds of stones, which tinge in a particular way. All fixed powders that have the power of tinging, I call Stones. The first and foremost of all Stones is the Philosopher's Stone; then comes the Tincture of the Sun and Moon in the white; then the

---

* As far as the heaven is from the earth, so far is the true Philosopher's Stone from this Fire Stone. I confess that though I have found the Fire Stone, I have yet much to learn concerning the more potent tincture.

Tincture of Vitriol or Venus; and also the Tincture of Mars. The two latter include the Tincture of the Sun. Then come the Tinctures of Jupiter and Saturn, for the coagulation of Mercury, and, finally, the Tincture of Mercury itself. All these different Tinctures are generated from <u>one original mother</u>, to which the great Universal Tincture also owes its birth; but apart from these there are no other tinctures. It is not, however, my business, in this place, to describe these tinctures or stones, because they have no medicinal value. The animal and vegetable Stones, indeed, have certain curative properties; but all these are contained and summed up in the great Philosopher's Stone.

The salts have no power of tinging, but are only keys in the preparation of the tinctures which we have named.*

---

* The salts open the chest in which the treasure is preserved, but are not themselves the treasure. You should, of course, distinguish between those salts which have a dissolving action, and those which coagulate and enter into the composition of the Stone—a distinction that is implied in the text.

Metallic salts should by no means be despised nor rejected in the preparation of the tincture, since they form an indispensable element in their composition ; for they contain the precious substance which is the cause of all fixation.

Next, the question arises whether the Stone can be prepared without a substance. The answer is in the negative, for everything must have its substance. Animals, vegetables, and minerals, have each their own particular first substance. But no substance can be of any use in the generation of our Stone without fermentation. From the tangible and formal body we must elicit the spiritual and celestial entity (I hardly know what expression to use in describing it). This entity, or essence, has first been infused into the body by stellar influences, and perfected and digested by the elements. By the digestion and regimen of the lesser fire, the spiritual entity must become a tangible, fixed, and solid substance.

But to what purpose do I speak,

and what do I say? I speak as one who has temporarily lost control over his organs of speech. If an atom of judgment still remained to me, I should not have opened my mouth so wide, and I should have stayed my hand, even at the last moment.*

All tinctures should be so prepared as to have an irresistible attraction towards the metals, and an irresistible inclination to mingle with them, and perfect them by removing their infirmities. It is the same as with human beings who are inflamed with mutual love, and cannot rest by day or night till they are brought together in loving union, and satisfy their desire; after that they rest, and multiplication takes place according to the order of Nature.

Man is subject to many grievous

---

* Are you in your right mind, Basilius, so to prostitute the Stone, which has hitherto been so carefully kept a secret by all the Sages? You have here let out the whole secret, and now we see how the pure and the impure are separated, how the fixed become volatile, and the volatile fixed. Now, you, my reader, attend carefully! There is here for you a precious pearl; do not resemble the fowl in the fable.

diseases, some of which so weaken and
impair his vitality that he cannot be re-
restored to perfect health by any means.
But love is a disease to which no other
disease can be compared, which can be
cured only by the production of its
counterpart ; nor is either of the two
natures satisfied until the desire of both
parts has met with fruition. Love assails
the young as well as the old, the poor as
well as the rich, the woman as well as
the man, and will take no denial. Those
whom it attacks it pervades, body, soul,
and spirit. In the heart it kindles a
torch, whose fire is diffused through the
veins, the arteries, and all the limbs of
the body. Where love once has struck
root it enslaves the whole man, and he
forgets God, heaven, hell, honour, the
present life and the life to come, in the
frenzied pursuit of his desire. Such a
person tramples underfoot the wise and
sober counsel of parents, and breaks loose
from all restraint. Love renders a man
blind, deaf, and dulls all other feelings
and thoughts ; it robs him of his sleep,

his appetite for food and drink, and renders him incapable of exercising prudent
forethought with regard to the future ; it
makes him forget his calling, vocation,
study, prayer.   If the lover does not obtain what he desires, or if his wishes are
not immediately fulfilled, by what melancholy, sorrow, and anguish is he tormented!   How soon he wastes away to
a mere shadow!   How often does he
not die of a broken heart!   In short,
such persons think very slightly either of
this life or of the life to come, until they
have been satisfied with the enjoyment
of the loved object.

But I, as a monk, must not dilate
any further upon the symptoms of this
unholy and consuming passion.   I have
kept myself pure from it all my life, and
pray God that He may preserve me
faithful to my holy spouse, the Church,
even to the end.   Even what I have
said was only mentioned for the purpose
of shewing by what passionate love the
tinctures should be violently attracted
towards their metals, in order that they

may penetrate them wholly, and thus bring them to perfection.

Our Stone is digested and matured by fire, like all things else that are found in this world. Nevertheless, different substances require different fires for their development.

The first fire is that of heaven, and quickens in our hearts love towards God our Father, and the Lord Jesus Christ our Saviour. The faith enkindled by this love can never forsake us in any trouble or distress.

Another fire is the elementary heat of the Sun, which brings everything in the great world to perfection.

The third fire is that corporal fire with which we cook our food and medicines—without which we could not maintain our health, or even our life. The fourth fire is that mentioned previously, which will one day consume the visible world. The fifth fire is the instrument of everlasting punishment, in which the devils and wicked men will be tormented for ever and ever. I exhort

o

all men to seek God, and to listen to His gracious voice while it may be heard, in order that they may escape from the terrible fire of hell.

Our Fire Stone should be prepared and matured, like our food and all other medicines, by the corporal fire which reigns in the little world. Where the solar fire of the great world leaves off, there our corporal fire begins a new generation. Corn grows and ripens by the heat of the great Fire; but a new process of cooking and maturing is brought about by the action of the little fire, in order that men may be able to use it for their bodily sustenance.

The oil of Antimony, from which our Fire Stone is prepared, is exceedingly sweet. It is rendered so brilliant by the removal of its earth, and of all impurities, that it may be compared to a bit of crystal on which the meridian rays of the sunshine fall. The method of its preparation is as follows :

Take, in the name of God, equal parts of the ore of Antimony, obtained

after sunrise, and of saltpetre ; pulverize
finely, mix well, place over a gentle fire,
bake dexterously (and the method of
this baking is the key of the whole
work). There will remain a blackish
substance. Out of this prepare glass,
which pound, extract its red Tincture
with strong distilled vinegar (made of the
same ore), and remove the vinegar by
distillation in the bath. There remains
a powder from which you should make a
second extract with highly rectified spirit
of wine. ' Let the fæces settle. You
have then a beautiful, sweet, red extract
of great medicinal value. This is the
pure Sulphur of Antimony. If you have
two pounds of this extract, take four
ounces of salt of Antimony (of which
I have given the receipt). Pour over
these the extract, circulate for at least a
month in a well-closed vessel, when the
salt will unite with the extract of sulphur ; remove sediment, if any, extract

---

* Take care at this point not to scorch the pinions of
your bird, which is already winging its flight above the
hills.

spirit of wine in S. Mary's Bath, sublime
the powder which remains, and it will
be distilled in the form of a many-
coloured, sweet, pellucid, reddish oil.
Rectify this oil in S. Mary's Bath, so
that the fourth part remains, and it is
then prepared.

Then take living Mercury of Antimony, which I have taught you how to
compose.* Pour to it red oil of vitriol,
made over iron, and highly rectified;
remove by distillation in sand the viscidity of the Mercury, and you will have
a precious precipitate of a glorious
colour, which is of the greatest medicinal
value in chronic diseases and open
wounds. For it quickly dries up their
symptomatic humours, which represent
the radical moisture of the disease.

Take equal parts of this precipitate
and of our sweet oil of Antimony; put
into a well-closed phial; if exposed to

---

* That is, the Mercury of the Sages so often alluded to.
Whoever tells you the secret of this Mercury will be your
Pylades, and you will be his Orestes. I, for my part,
shall be glad to make a third in such a company.

gentle heat, the precipitate will gradually
be dissolved and fixed in the oil : for the
fire consumes its viscidity, and it becomes
a red, dry, fixed, and fluid powder, which
does not give out the slightest smoke.*

When you have reached this point,
my friend, you have the Medicine of
men and of metals ; it is pleasant, sweet,
and penetrating, and may be used without any risk. Without being a purgative, it expels all impure and morbid
matter from the body. It will restore to
you health, and relieve you of want in
this life ; nor can you ever discharge to
God your obligation of gratitude for it.
I fear that as a monk and religious man
I have transcended the proper bounds of
reticence and secrecy, and spoken out
too freely.† At any rate, I have told

---

* Keep reverent silence : for now the King enters his
bridal chamber, where he will delight himself many
months with his spouse : and they will only leave the
chamber when they have grown together, and produced a
son who, if not the King of Kings, is at least a King, and
delivers his subjects from disease and want.

† Our Author fears that he has said too much. If you
share this opinion, his anxiety will be joy to you. It is
marvellous that when a Sage has thrown ever so little light
on this subject, he immediately regrets having done so.

you enough ; and if after all that has
been said you do not discover the secret,
it will not be my fault.

I have spoken as lucidly and openly,
nay, I fear, more openly, than the rules
of our brotherhood permit.　For it is
not lawful for every one to eat of the
Tree of Knowledge which stands in the
midst of Paradise.　I will now proceed
to describe the uses of this Elixir.

With reference to its medicinal
application to the human body, the dose
ought to be regulated and determined
by careful observation of individual
peculiarities of constitution.　Nevertheless, an excessive quantity is not really
dangerous, as there is no poison in our
Elixir.　Three or four grains at a time,
given in spirit of wine, are sufficient for
the cure of every disease ; for this
Medicine penetrates every part of the
body, and contains within itself the
potency of many arcana.　It removes
dizziness and all pulmonary complaints,
as well as coughs and all difficulty of
breathing.　It is a wonderful remedy for

leprosy and the French (venereal) disease. It cures the plague, dropsy, and all kinds of fevers, and constitutes a powerful antidote to poison. It invigorates the brain and the whole nervous system, the stomach, the liver, and the kidneys, breaks up the calculus and expels it, restores the vital spirits, promotes the menstrual discharge, removes barrenness both in men and women. Taken internally, and aided by suitable external plasters, it cures cancer, fistula, caries of the bones, and all corroding ulcers. In short, it relieves and finally removes all symptoms which indicate disease in the human body, as you will soon discover, if God has called you to be a physician.*

I have now told you all that I know about Antimony ; it is my prayer that

---

* You see Basilius speaks only of the medicinal virtues of this Fire Stone. For he assumes that you are chiefly inspired by the wish to help your suffering neighbour, and that you despise all sordid thoughts of filthy lucre. Farewell, gentle Reader, and if this Book has revealed to you the Grand Secret, shew your gratitude to God by kindly help rendered to your suffering brethren.

you may discover the rest, so that the fulness of God's wonderful gifts to men may be made known before the end of the world. I return to my Monastery, where I mean to devote myself to further study, and, if possible, to elucidate the secrets of vitriol, common sulphur, and the magnet, their origin, preparation, and virtues.

May the God and Lord of Heaven and Earth vouchsafe unto us health in time here, and hereafter salvation, with eternal rest to our souls, on thrones of joy and gladness, world without end! Amen.

Thus I conclude this Treatise on Antimony. Pay particular attention to what has been said of the red oil of Antimony, which is prepared from highly purified sulphur, and of the spirit which is prepared from its salt; compare these operations with what I have written concerning the Fire Stone, and then put the two together. For in this way you will run down the deer which you have been pursuing for so long.

INDEX.

Price Two Guineas.

In two volumes, small quarto, cloth extra, gilt.

The Hermetic Museum

Restored and enlarged, most faithfully instructing all the Disciples
of the Sopho-Spagyric Art how that Greatest and Truest Medicine
of the Philosopher's Stone may be found and held.

Now first done into English from the rare Latin original, published
at Frankfort in the year 1678. The illustrations reproduced in
fac-simile by a photographic process.

This curious storehouse of Hermetic Science comprises twenty-
two choice treatises on the Mysteries of Alchemy, and the composition of the Medicine of the Philosophers, namely :—

The Golden Treatise concerning the
Philosopher's Stone.
The Golden Age come back.
The Sophic Hydrolith, or Water
Stone of the Wise.
The Demonstration of Nature.
A Philosophical Summary.
The Path of the only Truth.
The Glory of the World, or Table
of Paradise.
The Generation of Metals.
The Book of Alze.
Figures and Emblems concerning the
Philosopher's Stone.
The Practice and Keys of Basil
Valentine.

The Ordinal of Alchemy.
The Testament of John Cremer, some-
time Abbot of Westminster.
The New Light of Alchemy.
The Sulphur of the Philosophers.
An Open Entrance to the Closed
Palace of the King.
A Subtle Allegory concerning the
Secrets of Chemistry.
The Metamorphosis of Metals.
A Short Guide to the Celestial Ruby.
The Fount of Chemical Truth.
The Golden Calf.
The All-Wise Doorkeeper.

While affording to the modern student of Hermetic Doctrines
an unique opportunity of acquiring in English a representative collection of the chief alchemical writers, this edition of THE
HERMETIC MUSEUM claims consideration at the hands of the
historian and archæologist as a contribution of real value to the
early history of chemistry. The translation is the work of a
gentleman who has had a life-long acquaintance with alchemical
literature, and has been subjected to careful revision by another
expert in Hermetic Antiquities.

N.B.—This Edition is limited to 250 copies, numbered and signed.

Now Ready.

Crown 8vo, printed from old-faced type, on antique laid paper,
cloth extra.   Price 10s. 6d.

A Golden and Blessed Casket of Nature's Marvels.

CONCERNING THE BLESSED MYSTERY OF THE PHILOSOPHER'S STONE.

Containing the Revelation of the Most Illuminated Egyptian King and Philosopher, Hermes Trismegistus : translated by our German Hermes, the Noble and Beloved Monarch and Philosopher Trismegistus, A. Ph. Theophrastus Paracelsus.   Also Tinctura Physicorum Paracelsica, with an excellent explanation by the Noble and Learned Philosopher, Alexander von Suchten, M.D., together with certain hitherto unpublished treatises by this author, and also other corollaries of the same nature as specified in the preface.   Now published for the use and benefit of all sons of the Doctrine of Hermes.

By BENEDICTUS FIGULUS, OF UTENHOFEN.

In Preparation.

Crown 8vo, printed from old-faced type, on antique laid paper, cloth
extra.   Price 10s. 6d.

Turba Philosophorum.

The most ancient of Western Treatises on Alchemy and the Great Work, the subject of continual reference by all later adepts, ranking second only to the writings of Hermes Trismegistus, and recognised as a final authority in the "practice of the philosophers."

While it has been the subject of innumerable commentaries and of the most pious veneration on the part of Hermetic students, this curious fountain-head of alchemical literature has never been previously translated.   A very careful version, containing both of the accepted recensions and the most important of the varied readings in the different printed editions, and in available manuscripts, is now preparing, and a limited number of copies will shortly be issued to the public.   The elucidations of selected commentators will be added to the text, and in the introduction prefixed to the work an attempt will be made to trace the history and influence of this archaic *Colloquium Sophorum.*

Crown 8vo, printed from old-faced type, on antique laid
paper, cloth extra, price 7s. 6d.

Collectanea Chemica:

Being certain select treatises on Alchemy and Hermetic
Medicine, by EIRENÆUS PHILALETHES, FRANCIS
ANTONY, GEORGE STARKEY, SIR GEORGE
RIPLEY, and ANONYMOUS UNKNOWN.

CONTENTS:

The Secret of the Immortal Liquor called Alkahest.
Aurum Potabile.
The Admirable Efficacy of the True Oil of Sulphur Vive.
The Stone of the Philosophers.
The Bosom Book of Sir George Ripley.
The Preparation of the Sophic Mercury.

The Hermetic Tracts comprised in this volume are
printed from a quarto manuscript belonging to the celebrated collection of the late Mr. Frederick Hockley, who
was well known among modern students of the secret
sciences not only for the resources of his Hermetic
Library, but for his practical acquaintance with many
branches of esoteric art, and for his real or reputed
connection with the numerous but unavowed associations
which now, as at anterior periods, are supposed to dis-
pense initiation into occult knowledge.

Crown 8vo, printed from old-faced type on antique laid paper, cloth extra, illustrated with symbolical designs, photographically reproduced.   Price 10s. 6d.

The Pearl of Great Price.

A NEW TREATISE CONCERNING THE TREASURE AND MOST PRECIOUS PHILOSOPHER'S STONE ;

Or the Method and Procedure of this Divine Art ; being observations drawn from the works of Arnold, Raymond, Rhasis, Albertus, and Michael Scotus. . Now first published by James Lacinius the Calabrian, with a copious Index.

Translated into English from the much-prized edition of Aldus, which appeared, with the privilege of Pope Paul III. and the Senate of Venice, in 1546.

The *Pretiosa Margarita Novella* is supposed to be a " faithful abridgment " of a work entitled *Margarita Pretiosa*, which appears to have circulated in manuscript in Italy during the first half of the fourteenth century, but does not seem to have been printed.   It was written by Pietro Bono, who enjoys high repute as an adept in the art of Alchemy ; and the present version, which has been subjected to a searching revision, is edited with an introductory analysis of the various Hermetic books which are attributed to this author.   The *Pretiosa Margarita Novella* has special interest as one of the earliest books which appeared in print on Alchemy.

www.ingramcontent.com/pod-product-compliance
Lightning Source LLC
Chambersburg PA
CBHW030407270326
41926CB00009B/1312